Gifting and the Stick

6-16-12

Boyd Keisel

Gifting and the Stick

Boyd Keisel

Gifting and the Stick
available now at mybkstories.com
or amazon.com

ISBN: 1519535988
ISBN 13: 9781519535986
Gifting and the Stick: True stories of life lessons with America's Greatest Generation.
1, Utah—Memoir—Anecdotes. 2. Choices—Consequences—Humor. 3. Difference Makers--Becoming
Library of Congress Control Number: 2015919848
CreateSpace Independent Publishing Platform
North Charleston, South Carolina

Contents

Acknowledgments

I COULD NOT have written this collection of stories without the encouragement and untold hours my wife, Natalie, spent at the computer. Thanks also to the many family members, friends, and strangers who told me, "We need stories like these—stories that in these tumultuous times remind us of our rich heritage."

To the Reader

THE STORIES YOU'RE about to read are mine. But, more than that, they tell about the difference makers—those who made do and then gave back. These accounts, written over many years, are a testament to the power and strength of family. They speak of the virtues of love and sacrifice, of overcoming life's challenges.. As snapshots of life with America's Greatest Generation, these stories offer a glimpse into a time and place where the resiliency of the human spirit—and truth and wisdom—was often found in unexpected places.

The men and women we've come to know as America's Greatest Generation shouldered the harsh consequences of the Great Depression, World War II, and the Korean War. Certain in their faith in a loving God, they gifted us with possibility and hope, the same forces that sustained them as they overcame the ravages of war, loss of loved ones, and a world in turmoil. They understood that their own happiness and well-being could not exist at the expense of others and lived life accordingly.

Casting shadows from the past, these stories point the way to the future, teaching that opposition is a blessing, a necessity for growth. Rooted in the customs and heritage of a farming and ranching community of some fifteen hundred citizens in Ephraim, Utah, the stories speak of the sometimes-harsh and often-humorous realities of life and of the need to laugh at ourselves along the way.

Perhaps more than anything, these stories bear witness to the fact that into each life will come a few defining moments, experiences, and individuals with the ability to leave us more empowered than they found us. The only question, then, is this: Will we seize the moment and see more of who we are and how to be? This often requires looking past the judgment of our eyes to discover the potential of those who generally aren't thought to have any. You'll meet some of these people within these pages.

To the best of my recollection, the stories in this book are true with respect to the people, times, and events they portray. They appear here as they unfolded from the pages of my memory. I either lived the stories myself or, as is the case with a few of them, relied on memories of tales told to me by others. On occasion, I've assigned pseudonyms to protect the privacy of certain individuals; however, for the most part, I've used actual names and nicknames. Some of those people—the ones I call the Difference Makers—changed the course of my life in significant ways.

Finally, I must confess that I never intended to write a book. I just wanted my family to know about the people and experiences that shaped much of who I am. The stories in this work are a reflection of the lives from which they came—a record of sorts, written through a window of time, bringing light to a community's rich heritage. As you read, I hope you'll discover and acknowledge our similarities, flaws, failures, and successes and find reasons to smile a bit in the face of the fires of life. Enjoy!

Introduction

TWO SETS OF experiences inspired the title of this collection of stories. The first came to me as I rubbed shoulders with an aging trapper. "Little Joe" had ties to the Lakota Sioux and often talked about how he'd been "gifted" with so many blessings over his long life.

The second resulted from listening to a traditional Navajo grandmother counsel a wayward granddaughter about the wisdom and consequences of her choices. "Pick up one end of the stick, and you pick up the other," the grandmother admonished.

Some insights only reveal themselves as we progress through the school of life. Wisdom, purpose, and understanding are a few examples. Sometimes these threads of life come into our lives quickly. However, as with so many of life's lessons, acquiring such knowledge more often than not takes time, distance, and perhaps a fresh set of eyes before these threads become a part of us.

Some of these threads were called "Gifting" and "the Stick" by early Native American elders who wanted to guide their people to a better life. To the Lakota Sioux, the "Gifting" way of life pointed to a set of values and behaviors that taught people to avoid being too self-centered. This way of life is about sharing—lifting others up and being our brothers' keepers. Gifting warns that we should not become too attached to things, a practice that often leads to greed and pride.

"The Stick," a Navajo allegory of wisdom regarding choices and consequences, teaches us that when we pick up one end of a stick, we pick up the other, meaning that our choices—the end of the stick we pick up—have consequences waiting at the other end. Simply put, good choices return that which is good, while poor choices beget that which is poor.

My mom, dad, and all the Difference Makers in my life were constantly engaged in the traditions of Gifting and the Stick. As parents of fourteen children, Mom and Dad were challenged in many ways as they provided for and guided their flock down life's pathways.

Truly a woman of humility and honor, Mom gifted us with the blessings of those virtues through steadfast example. Dad took us to the mountains, where he taught us to love all God's creatures, great and small. He spoke with quiet conviction about how insignificant he felt while gazing up at the heavens on a clear night, gifting us with the sure knowledge of God's hand in our lives. Maybe one of his greatest gifts was instilling in us, by example, the blessing of work and of earning our own way in the world.

To that end, Mom was the hardest, humblest worker I've ever known. Even though she had so many children, she often cared for others outside the family as well, paying attention to their health and spiritual well-being. I remember asking Mom why she continued doing so as the years and her own health issues took their toll. Her reply was simple: "Because I should and can." She paused and then continued, "It's only right that I should give back a little of what I've been blessed with." It was her way of showing compassion and service to family members, friends, neighbors, and strangers. If there was a need, Mom was always there.

When it came to applying the allegory of the Stick, Dad had his own translation. I well remember his words after I told a fib or filched an egg or two from the coop, intending to trade them for candy. "Roll around in the muck with the pigs, and you're sure to come out smelling like one," he would say, scolding me.

Another time, as I tell in the story "Choices and Consequences," I chose to violate an agreement with my high-school basketball coach. Mom pointed out my transgression, and I clearly got the message: "Pick up one end of the stick, and I'll see to it that you pick up the other end." She taught a life lesson while quietly holding my feet to the fire.

Given the benefit of time, distance, and experience (some of which I learned in the School of Hard Knocks), I now see more clearly what the Gifting and the Stick principles are about. They give us a road map to a better, more honest way of life, allowing us to understand and realize a sense of purpose greater than ourselves. Knowing, however, isn't enough. We must be *doers*. Only then will we and those we serve *do* more and *be* more.

Gifting and the Stick do not weave the cloth of life independent of each other, as it is the power of Gifting that can turn picking up the wrong end of the stick and the hard consequences that follow those choices into blessings. The story "More Than Words" shows an example of a bad choice becoming a gift.

Finally, as you read the stories that follow, you will see how Gifting and the Stick are principles that have become a way of life for me, and hopefully they will weave themselves into your own life as well. I hope that embracing the powers of Gifting and the Stick will leave you feeling empowered and enlightened during your life's journey. But remember, just watching isn't enough: *doing* is the key!

An Early Spring

With a second look comes a new perspective.

How does the stuff of life get started? It's a question whose answer seems both simple and complex. Take the changing of the seasons, for example. Every few months, so it seems, the change just *happens*. In reality, though, a lot of big stuff is happening every day, and then, almost magically, it is spring or summer, fall or winter. Yet until the forces of change have moved far enough, the change is barely noticeable.

When you think about it, the seasons—the stuff of life—never move independently of their parts. It's all a giant constellation dancing to the music of time, motion, space, and unseen forces. For some of God's creatures, the dance is short and fast. For others, the music plays to deaf ears until some event, some force, aligns its parts and creates a new season, a new awareness, and a new melody.

For me, the eighth-grade dance was that event. Until then, I knew boys and girls were different, but girls, I thought, were merely to be tolerated. Somewhere in my brief existence, I had recognized, vaguely, that men and women were eventually supposed to get together. In the meantime, girls were just there, and according to Mom, Dad, and the teachers, we boys had to simply accept them, at the very least.

I didn't have a lot of trouble doing that; I just ignored girls most of the time. But then one day, someone decided that the eighth-grade boys and girls ought to smooth out the rough spots of their relationships.

We boys knew something big was afoot when the girls came out of Miss Mansfield's classroom hugging one another and giggling. They looked at Bob, a good-looking kid with big muscles and curly hair, as if he were a double-decker ice-cream cone on a hot summer day. They didn't look at *me* that way. I got the same old "get lost" stares, if they even looked my way at all.

That was all right with me, but it wasn't all right with Miss Mansfield. She was determined to "civilize" everyone—with no exceptions! Even then, the irony of Miss Mansfield's leading this expedition into puberty wasn't lost on the male segment of my class.

From a physical standpoint, Miss Mansfield was the spitting image of Popeye's girlfriend, Olive Oyl. But personality-wise, she never smiled at boys and always appeared tight-lipped. I don't remember ever seeing the corners of her mouth turn up—except when she made *the announcement*.

"Beginning Monday, during phys-ed class, we will practice for the eighth-grade dance. When you've learned the proper etiquette and steps, we'll invite Manti's eighth graders to join us." (Manti was a neighboring town seven miles to the south.) The reaction was immediate: the girls gasped with joy, and Bob sank into his seat along with the rest of the boys.

I started to protest. "If we have to, can't we practice during *this* class? Why do we have to do it in PE?"

"Oh, we'll practice here." Miss Mansfield assured me. "You'll learn how to treat our girls like they deserve to be treated. When I get through with you, you'll be worthy of the opportunity to at least ask our girls to dance with you! Not only that, we're going to have a dinner. You gentlemen"—she got a strange glow in her eyes when she said that—"will learn to conduct our ladies to the dinner table, to seat them, and to properly consume a meal in their presence."

I leaned over and asked Dave what "consume" meant. He didn't know either, but Gary told us it meant "to eat."

"Geez," I moaned, "she must be from another planet. Crap, I know how to eat!"

At least I thought I did. But I was to learn that there was eating my way, then there was *proper* eating, and beyond that there was eating according to Miss Mansfield. "Civilized dining," she called it. "Dining with proper respect for the ladies," Miss Mansfield said.

One of our first classroom lessons was learning the rudiments of seating a lady. The big affair was to start off with a grand entry into the dining hall, where each gentleman was to take a lady on his arm, escort her to the assigned table, and position her chair properly so that she could be seated with dignity.

That wasn't too hard to master, but after four or five dry runs, the boredom was more than my friend Cob Greaves could handle. He'd been watching Molly, my partner for the grand entry, go through her paces. Now, by any stretch of the imagination, Molly wasn't going to be light on her feet. She carried 220 pounds on her five-foot-four-inch frame and shuffled forward one side at a time. The only time she moved everything at once was when she took her seat. Once her descent to the chair began, there was no holding her back; only the seat could halt the free fall.

I had dutifully moved the chair back—a long way back—to make room. Molly brought her right side and then her left into position in front of the chair. I stepped to the back of the chair, where it would be my duty to assist Molly in moving the chair forward to the proper position at the table once she was seated. But in the split second between Molly's descent and impact, Cob, unable to resist, jerked the chair away. And Molly came down—all the way down!

With my own survival at stake, I leaped abruptly away. That was a mistake. I would have been better off being squashed underfoot like a ripe plum. The "seismograph" recorded the impact at 2.3, and I think the aftershock was 4.5 on the Richter scale. The latter was *me* bouncing off the walls on the way to the principal's office.

The "code" demanded that I not rat on my friend Cob. Also, it occurred to me that I might be "excused" from the dance, so I dummied up and prepared to take my medicine.

But after an appropriate amount of yelling and cussing, it was determined that I needed this training more than ever, and what happened next was right out of *Ripley's Believe It or Not*.

To cover up and divert attention away from himself, Cob had leaped to Molly's aide. He assisted her up and inquired about her health. He hovered over her and made sure Miss Mansfield knew of his "concern."

Miss Mansfield was duly impressed.

"What we need around here are more gentlemen like Cob!" she informed the class. "Cob, you and Boyd change partners. I know you'll want to make sure Molly is treated with the respect she deserves. Your concern is to be admired!"

Now *that* was the trade of the century. Molly for Nancy! I'd always kind of liked Nancy, and she seemed to think I was her friend. At least she treated me that way. Besides, she was a cheerleader type.

At the end of the first day's practice with Nancy, it occurred to me that maybe this eighth-grade dance wouldn't be so bad; there could be some benefits. A day or two later, I found myself at home in my upstairs bedroom, practicing the two-step in front of the large mirror on the wall. The broom I held was a great follower, and I hardly ever stepped on its toes.

The next day, Nancy commented to me, "You're a good dancer." That was it! I went into two-a-day at-home practices—morning and night. In my imagination, the broom became Nancy, and we danced as one. I visualized spending the entire dance sweeping her off her feet. I worked really hard to get everything down just right. And while I still didn't like Miss Mansfield, I had a disturbing thought: *Maybe this whole idea isn't so bad after all.*

The days flew by, and finally the big night arrived. I took a bath twice that day—that was one bath more than I usually took in a week—and put on my new shirt and my dad's tie. Cob had by that time forgiven me for my good fortune and had shown me how to tie it. I also borrowed some Vitalis and Old Spice from my big brother. The Vitalis made my hair lie down like Humphrey Bogart's. I put a dash of Old Spice on my cheeks and saturated each armpit a couple of times for good measure. When I left the house, I noticed Old Skip, our three-legged dog, whimper and disappear around the corner of the house, tail between his legs. I'd seen that behavior once before when he stuck his nose under a hay pile occupied by a skunk.

At school, we lined up in the hall with our partners and escorted them to the cafeteria for a dinner of ham, mashed potatoes, corn, and green Jell-O. You couldn't have a dinner without it! We were joined by the eighth-grade class from Manti. After dinner, we walked our partners to the old gym, and on the way there, I wondered how it was that some of the girls looked so pretty. I mean, they hadn't ever looked that way before. Not only that but also Nancy was surely the prettiest, and I felt kind of light-headed.

The old gym had been decorated, and proud parents and grandparents filled the bleachers. We marched into the gym and circled the floor twice so the spectators could get a good look at the spectacle. It was a grand affair! Miss Mansfield's eyes glowed, but no smile was to be seen on her face. I thought she was glaring at me the whole time.

The first dance would be with our partners, the ones we'd practiced with. When the music began, Nancy smiled at me, and we glided around the floor. I didn't step on her toes once, and she seemed to move a little closer. I was happy about all the Old Spice under my armpits. It was awfully warm in there.

When the music stopped, we all went back to our places in the circle. Then, while the girls stood still, the boys marched forward until we were paired up with someone from the other school. We introduced ourselves as we'd been taught, and the music from the old phonograph came to life.

I don't remember much about that dance, or the other girls I danced with; I was too busy watching Nancy. Man, she sure seemed to be enjoying herself with that kid from Manti.

The music ended, and the girls were escorted to their seats in the first two rows of bleachers on the south side of the gym. All the boys then took a seat on the north side.

When the music started up again, the boys were to approach the girls of their choice and request a dance. I headed for Nancy, but before I got to her, three other boys appeared before her, and off she went into the crowd. That scene repeated itself again and again. After every dance, the floor cleared, and when the music signaled "go," the lineup of boys awaiting Nancy's favor grew longer. After three or four futile attempts, I gave up and slipped out the back door.

On that crisp, clear May evening, I pulled my tie off and thought, *That feels good. Heck, I'd just as soon go magpie hunting anyway.* "In fact," I said out loud, "with all the magpie hunting and fishing I'll be doing, I won't have time for Nancy anyway. Girls just get in the way of that kind of stuff."

It was a convincing argument, but I could still smell Nancy's cologne. I went home and took another bath. Old Skip seemed to accept that as a sign of apology and wagged his tail as I walked by him. Those few days with Nancy were like an early spring thaw. They couldn't last long in that time, place, and season of my life. It was too early for the buds and blossoms of young love to flower. Yet like the February thaw, they offered a promise of things to come—of a time, place, and season when my path would merge with that stranger, that still-unknown girl, who would bring the warmth of summer into my life.

Until then, what I had was enough. My universe, my season, was basketball and hunting, fishing, and other kinds of boy stuff. To everything there is a season. Nancy was, after all, just a girl.

Rites of Passage

The ability to choose wisely is to know when to say when.

Becoming a teenager in my hometown in rural Utah meant that boy-girl stuff was about to happen. Not that I didn't know there was something different about girls. I did. But until eighth grade, I thought girls were, well, just different. Most of them just liked to do schoolwork and please their teachers.

To make matters worse, half the girls in my class were bigger, faster, and stronger than the boys. They could make life miserable without even trying. For example, our physical-education teachers decided that tumbling would be something eighth graders ought to experience. At that time, girls took part in cheerleading, drill-team competitions, and gymnastics, but you didn't see boys engaging in those activities; most boys worked hard to ignore and avoid these. They just didn't seem manly and were classified as "sissy" stuff.

Besides, those pursuits were just examples of ways in which girls could make life miserable if boys entered their realm. I had a bad feeling about that tumbling thing from the beginning. I was skinny, gangly, and uncoordinated. Next thing I knew, some of the girls were talking about putting on a program for the parents to showcase their cartwheels, flips, and rolls. Before the boys could organize and protest, the show was on. Compounding the problem, an edict came down from the teachers: *Everyone had to take part!*

Now, that little development would give birth to the ultimate embarrassment of my young and tender life. Because I was a sure disaster as far as flips and rolls were concerned, I became the "catch man" for the forward flip. My job was to lie on my back on the mat, my knees up and feet planted firmly on the mat. Then, my classmates lined up under the basket at the other end of the floor and ran, one at a time, full speed to my location at midcourt, where they dove forward, placing a hand on each of my knees with their head pointed toward the floor. Their momentum brought their feet up. I propelled them into a spectacular spinning forward roll by catching them on their shoulders and lifting. Their hands and my knees were pivot points for the launch.

Remember I said earlier that the girls were bigger, stronger, and faster? Well, one girl in particular was *a lot* bigger. It was Molly! During rehearsals, I had real problems getting her up and over. This girl wasn't bigger, stronger, and faster; she was just *bigger*!

When she came down the runway, even though I couldn't see her at first, the vibration of the floor signaled her approach. And more often than not, my knees flew open and my arms collapsed at the moment of impact.

After being flattened several times and having to extract my nose from beneath her sweat-filled armpit an equal number of times, I decided that enough was enough; my very survival was at stake. And so it was that the natural, God-given instinct for self-preservation took over when the thunder and vibration coupled with sucking gasps for breath signaled Molly's approach. I looked between my knees and saw the determined eyes and sweat-drenched face; her mouth pulled back at the corners as the distance closed. I looked left, then right, and quick as a lightning bolt, sheer panic took over. One roll, two rolls, and into the fetal position I went!

I was later told that the windows rattled, the lights swayed, and the floor shook with the force of Molly's landing. My first impression as I lay tucked tightly in the fetal position, eyes closed, was that I'd been killed. There was no noise—just total silence! I dared not breathe. I dared not look.

Then a thunderous bellow echoed forth from the vicinity of the mat I'd just vacated. If I wasn't dead, I had a sinking feeling that I'd soon wish I were. Peeking between the fingers covering my face, I saw Miss Olsen and Coach Graser rushing in to assess the damage. The coach stopped at Molly's side, and Miss Olsen, her mouth tight and her eyes squinting, charged right by and latched onto my hair. I sprang up to my feet and landed in her office before I touched the ground again. As I said, girls were bigger, faster, and stronger then.

I don't recall much of the conversation that ensued. However, I remember that, for a week afterward, the boys all looked at me with hero worship. I'd done something—although purely instinctive—that none of them had dared to do. I had zapped Molly!

Life was good, but the euphoria quickly faded. The day of the program was too close to find and train another "catch man," and I was thrust back into action. Worse still, Molly was more determined than ever to demonstrate her "graceful" skills.

We all got white shorts and blue T-shirts for the occasion. The bleachers were filled as we went into our routines, and there were a lot of "oohs" and "aahs" from the crowd. Miss Olsen and Coach Graser were beaming with satisfaction at what they'd accomplished.

I took my place on the mat, and the first six of my classmates charged down the runway, planted their hands on my knees, and were thrust into graceful somersaults topped off with a series of forward rolls, landing upright on their feet. Each took a bow and stepped aside.

Suddenly, the crowd went deathly quiet. The floor shook, and I braced myself. Molly was coming! "Dear God," I prayed. I saw the eyes, the tight lips, and then the ceiling lights blotted from view as Molly dove for the target. Her sweaty palms locked on my knees and then slipped off. My arms collapsed under the burden, and her head plunged deep into my belly button.

The result was immediate. The air from my lungs was released in a whooshing, grunting sound. Another much louder and smellier form of air, unable to escape by way of my throat, exited my body by the only avenue available. This was capped off by two belch-like releases that reverberated and echoed through the still air of the gym.

I don't remember much about what followed that day, but I decided that since there had been two of us near the source of the offending noises, I would admit to nothing in the incident, which became known as "the second shot heard around the world"!

The Tyro Club

Image is only the first thing seen—one slice of the whole.

Growing up in rural Utah in the 1940s and '50s was a journey that only now is beginning to make sense. Sometimes learning is like that. The traveler on the path of life needs time, distance, and perspective to unravel the threads—time to examine, distance to reflect, and perspective to add up the parts, to see the entirety of the fabric of life.

The church, schools, and social and political structures of my hometown of Ephraim, Utah, were quite visible. They were the acknowledged power bases, the places where things were either blessed or damned. As was the case in nearly every town and city in Utah, the Mormon influence prevailed. The business establishments along Main Street were owned by Mormons, the political offices were filled by Mormons, and the schools were staffed by Mormons.

But there was an equally influential, equally active social order with its "corporate offices" wheeling and dealing. That was the membership of the Tyro Club. The Tyro Club had a regular clientele who came and went, for the most part, on a schedule you could set your watch by. The old pool hall attracted farmers, ranchers, merchants, doctors, and lawyers; winos and drifters; and young men who *would be* doctors, dentists, and educators. Even an occasional woman or two.

Community status, wealth, and ignorance were freely shared at the old bar, where a dozen or so stools fronted its mahogany top, worn smooth by the elbows of thirsty loggers, turkey farmers, truckers, and pool players. It was a place where a young man could learn a lot about life.

Maybe that's why the place was named the Tyro Club. "Tyro," according to the dictionary, means "a beginner in learning." But I don't think a lot of Tyro's customers knew that or gave a damn, for that matter. Nevertheless, the name gave the old place a sense of dignity even if its membership could not—not openly, anyway.

That was one of the mysteries of life in my hometown in the '50s that puzzled me. How was it that the same people who went to church together on Sunday had such differing views on life?

They'd all heard the same message. They all took the same vows. They all read and studied the same scriptures. And, for the most part, they cared for and looked out for each other.

There were, however, those who passed heavy judgment on others who failed to live the letter of religious dogma as they perceived it. When frequenting the Tyro Club, one might feel a cold chill in their presence.

Bart Thorpe owned the Tyro Club in the beginning. A small, bespectacled man—he was a keen observer of humanity. "I've seen 'em all," he told me one day. "One thing I've learned is that it's dangerous to pass judgment. Life takes some funny turns. Some roads lead to good places, others to not-so-good places."

He went on. "The thing is, just because a person is on one road today doesn't mean he'll be on the same road tomorrow."

So true! There's a powerful lesson in that statement. Recognition of its truth is what separates pseudoreligious practice from the real thing. The Lord's judgment is always tempered with forgiveness.

"Respect," Bart said, "is important in any belief system. It lies at the center of a person's relationship to nature and to the Creator, whatever you perceive Him to be. You look at the people who come in here. They're a pretty good cross-section of our town. You can tell a lot about them by the way they treat old Deaf Johnny."

Deaf Johnny was not, I suspect, far from the bottom of the town's social ladder. He liked to drink his share of beer and was careless about his appearance. Tobacco juice stained his teeth, his chin, and his shirt. Yet in the Tyro Club, Johnny was a member in good standing. Most patrons extended him a certain amount of respect—respect earned because he showed a tolerance and understanding for the few who attempted to belittle his circumstances.

One of my favorite Bible scriptures from the King James Version goes like this: "Inasmuch as ye have done it unto one of the least of these my brethren, ye have done it unto me" (Matt. 25:40). Deaf Johnny gave those of the Tyro Club ample opportunity to demonstrate that principle. It's one that can make us better *individuals* as we travel down life's pathways—especially when we encounter those less fortunate.

All learning doesn't take place in school. On any given Saturday afternoon, trucks driven by farmers, ranchers, and the rest of the "membership" lined Main Street. If the member happened to be important in the political or religious structure of the community, you might find the vehicle parked around the corner or over at Bill Nielson's service station. Some wives, concerned with social appearances, gave members cause to park in those places as well.

On one occasion, a loving wife brought a dinner tray to the table at which her husband had been engaged in a day-long card game. She smiled sweetly and placed the covered tray on the felt-top table next to her startled husband.

"Thought you might be getting hungry," she said kindly as she gave him a little peck on his forehead. All eyes were on her, and the place got very quiet as she exited with a flourish.

The look of apprehension on the husband's face changed to a smirk of satisfaction as he remarked, "See, boys! Ya just gotta train 'em right!" The membership had seen a few wild-eyed wives and girlfriends extract their men from those premises, but they were in awe of what they'd just witnessed.

"Probably steak and French fries," said the woman's husband, bragging. "And a big slice of hot apple pie!"

With that, he pulled the tray toward him and removed its linen cover. Again, there was total silence as the envious eyes of the onlookers followed every movement with anticipation. When the tray was uncovered, the hero's face suddenly went ash gray and then turned bright red. The whole place erupted in raucous laughter.

"Steak and fries and hot apple pie!" they cackled.

On the tray were two items: a bowl of dog food and a container filled with hot water. The message was clear—unmistakable. It shouted with no mercy: "You are in the doghouse, up to your hip pockets in hot water!"

Remember the definition of "tyro"? Well, the membership wasn't stupid. Maybe a little slow, but not stupid. One by one, two by two, the club emptied. In the space of ten minutes or so, the only clientele left were a couple of bachelors and the bartender.

"Tyro: A beginner in learning." The membership had demonstrated that they'd seen the light, and on this occasion they were past the "beginner" stage.

A lot of money changed hands at the Tyro Club. Pool players and card players wagered not only on their own skills but also on the skills of others. The club was a regular pit stop for players from a hundred miles away. While the players might bet a hundred dollars on themselves, their supporters also placed bets with each other. When the local "shark" and the visiting hustler got together, it wasn't unusual for hundreds of dollars to change hands in one evening. The payments were often referred to as "devil's tithing" or "learners' fees." Many a "frog skin" (dollar bill) changed hands with men who attended to their church duties the next day, richer or poorer for the experience.

Gambling has always been illegal in Utah and frowned upon by the dominant church. The goings-on at the Tyro Club, however, seemed immune to any such consequences. Perhaps the law felt that the women's power over their men was sufficient punishment. At any rate, local law enforcement drifted in and out of the place unnoticed by those who exchanged wagers and payoffs.

It cost four bits an hour for a pool table. A glass of draft beer was ten cents, but there was no cost for a chair at the half-dozen card tables on the balcony. Pickled eggs and wieners went for twenty cents each and led to a lot of coughing and teary eyes. If the consumers of these delights stayed around long enough, there were sure to be dangerous levels of methane released into the atmosphere, and one could identify the source by observing the distance between members. Isolation was a dead give-away during an attack of nonlethal gas.

Punchboards were big at that time, too. There were nickel, dime, and quarter boards. You could win a lot of good stuff, like peanuts, candy, knives, guns, and other useful gadgets. The members of the Tyro Club kept a watchful eye on the boards, and some with money got bargains. When the board was used up to a certain point, they would buy it out if the prizes that remained justified it.

A lot of business was conducted at the Tyro, too. Crops were bought and sold. Land was sold or leased, and livestock was traded and sold. Men were hired, and jobs contracted. Most of the transactions were sealed with a handshake and a man's word. That was enough in those days, when respect and trust were sometimes all a man had. It wasn't unusual for the owner of the Tyro to ask one of the customers to take over while he ran home or went to the bank for half an hour. That told me a lot about the members and the unwritten code. You didn't cheat. If you did, you didn't belong. And belonging was important.

When I was barely twenty, I left my home in the Sanpitch Valley. The Korean War was calling The draft board said it was my turn to give two years to my country. It was a cold January day, and Mom and Dad took me to the Trailways bus stop in Manti. I'd said my good-byes at home with my younger brothers and sisters. We stopped by Grandma and Grandpa Keisel's for a minute or two, and I got the same advice from my grandpa that I'd heard before when my two older brothers went off to war: "Remember who you are! Come back in one piece!"

Half an hour later, I heard my dad repeat those words. I gave Mom a hug and boarded the half-empty bus. We headed north past the old homestead, where my brothers and sisters stood at the roadside waving, through the main street of my hometown, and out of the Sanpitch Valley.

I'd been out of the sanctuary of the Sanpitch before, but this time was different. I was alone. I was beginning a journey with a lot of unknowns. My experiences at the Tyro Club and the lessons learned in the fields and mountains were to serve me well, as they had with my five brothers, in serving our country.

Two years later, I reentered the Sanpitch Valley. It was cold and dark, near midnight, and snow was falling. No one met me at the bus stop. Word hadn't come through that I was back in the States and finished with my tour of duty. We didn't have a phone, and the streets were deserted. Still, I thought I could find someone at the Tyro to take me the mile south of town and home.

I shouldered my heavy duffel bag and walked south toward the Tyro Club, only to find it dark and the doors closed. There was nothing to do but go on and make my way home on foot, as I'd done so many times before. I didn't mind the driving wind and snow. It was good to be home.

Later I would find out that the Tyro Club had changed owners and had moved to a new location. This event, like so many others along life's path, was to change the face of my hometown. The membership drifted away, and a chapter in time came to an end. As someone once observed, "One door closes, and another opens." Step through it, and life goes on, but always with lessons of the past to give birth to "a beginner in learning"—a tyro.

Third Grade

Make a blissful pit stop every day.

THIRD GRADE. FOR some unknown reason, recently my thoughts have been drifting back through the misty cobwebs of childhood memories. Some of the pages are blank. Some are full. When the full pages come to mind, it's because someone said something or I saw something to remind me of days past. Driving down Main Street in Manti, Utah, I went past the old Legion Hall, the place at which I attended school in third grade. We learned about the three Rs in this old building.

However, it was in the outhouse that we got our "education." Located next to a grove of plum trees, the outhouse stood fifty yards behind the Legion Hall. It was a duplex design, a wooden structure with boys to the left, girls to the right, and a two-holer on each side—a four-hole capacity separated by a board wall in the middle. The designer had been inspired to accommodate individual differences with holes sized to fit—big bottoms on the left, small stuff on the right.

Even then there were "outhouse poets." By Thanksgiving, all the boys could recite the single verse inscribed on the back of the wooden door by heart:

Isaac, Isaac, king of the Pews...Wiped his ass on the Deseret News. The paper was thin and his finger slipped in...I'd hate to be in the fix poor Isaac was in!

—THE OUTHOUSE POET

Word among the kids was that the "poet" had been expelled. Some said he had a job at the *Messenger*, the local weekly. Others referred to our third-grade teacher as "Isaac." Maybe all this explains why in some circles the place is called "the Reading Room."

I don't think outhouses get the credit and dignity they deserve. That's because they meet the most basic of our needs. We can't worry about or concentrate on the three *R*s, the pretty girl sitting up front in the classroom, or anything else when "needing to go" is our motivation. That's why on occasion, when we try to ignore "going," we find ourselves running for it! It's a race that can have dire consequences for one's status and reputation. Maybe that's why some call the place the restroom. Holding your breath while sprinting for relief can create a need for "resting."

On the other hand, I suspect that those old outhouses were the forerunners of modern restrooms with their magazine racks. We were more versatile then; we read the Sears & Roebuck or Montgomery Ward catalogs and then extracted a page for cleanup. Come to think of it, those catalogs were the first sex-education books. You could learn a lot by studying the ladies' lingerie section, which was always the last part of the book to go.

The old four-holer had its advantages and disadvantages. You could sit next to a friend, so you didn't get lonesome. But that caused twice the air pollution. It was a great place to eavesdrop on the girls' conversations, but you couldn't leave until the coast was clear. After all, it would be embarrassing to be identified with the sounds of "resting" or "reading" that reverberated from the common receptacle below.

The outhouse was good for learning, too. When students had to go, they didn't stay long on the cold seat on a frigid winter's day. The walk to the outhouse in the brisk air tended to clear your mind and enhance learning. If you happened to stay a little too long, you could always say you were "reading." What kind of teacher would object to that?

When the warm spring sun touched the grove of plum-bush blossoms, swarms of flies, bees, and hornets gathered there behind the outhouse. From there it was only a short flight to the four-holer, where they dipped and darted their way under the door and through crescent moon–shaped ventilation holes on the side walls. For the most part, the occupants and the winged creatures coexisted in tranquil peace.

Legend has it that one day, as a teacher was blissfully occupying the big hole, flies were enjoying the visit and gathering in large numbers around, over, and under. With each methane release, the swarm lifted away on the downdraft and then settled back for more as the teacher marveled at the verse of the Outhouse Poet. But, like a lot of parties, this one was about to be visited by a "party pooper"—a hornet, who buried its stinger deep in the left cheek of the big hole's occupant.

Vacating the premises, the teacher was heard to exclaim, "Dammit! Just for that, you can all get off!" That hornet became an instant hero among the students. Personally, I admire hornets. That's something I learned in third grade.

It seems like we lost an important link with our past when we moved the outhouse indoors. The old two-holer and four-holer have given way to the one-holer, and chamber pots don't sit under the bed anymore. We've created a distance in our relationships.

Somehow it doesn't seem as honest when we call it the john, restroom, ladies' or men's room, or bathroom. I have to admit, however, that "thinking room" has a certain ring to it. But then, so does "thunder mug." The Outhouse Poet could surely have done something with those monikers.

I think the move from outside to inside was inevitable. But I'm glad I experienced the outhouse in third grade before the EPA came along. How would you write a his-and-hers environmental-impact statement for a four-holer?

Thirteenth Summer

Experience and trust are tough taskmasters.

During the summer before my thirteenth birthday, things at home were much as they had been for each of the twelve previous summers. The food supply from the previous harvest was exhausted, yet the new crop was painfully slow in maturing.

The only things that seemed to spring up on our acre-sized family garden were the red roots and the morning glories, and even they had their place in the struggle to feed the family. Every weed pulled from the ground was carried to the pigpen, where two or three brood sows and their young devoured them. Since few scraps fell from the family table, the weed diet had to be maintained. The past summer's grain and hay supply had, like the winter's snow, disappeared with the spring thaw.

As had been the case in each of my previous summers, Dad had left home, joined Ed Chappel's crew, and was somewhere in Montana shearing sheep. It was during these times that everyone watched the mail for a letter from him in the hopes that a few dollars would be included, thereby giving us some cash to resupply our empty cupboards.

And while my younger brothers and sisters weren't aware of it, we older kids saw the pain in Mom's eyes as day after day one of us returned from the daily trip to the post office empty-handed.

Years later, I would learn that often the letters didn't arrive because there was simply no money. No money because Dad had been unlucky at cards or had gone to town while the sheep dried from a recent rainstorm and lost himself in a gallon of cheap wine. It wasn't something he wanted to do; it just happened. And then things got worse.

Being nearly thirteen, I began to feel some hints of social rejection, but only in subtle, little ways. After all, we were a family of fourteen children living in poverty, with an alcoholic father, who was absent each spring and summer.

I would fully understand only years later that prejudice was alive and well in some quarters of my hometown and that it had been a major force in shaping my existence. As a teenager, however, I thought it was just because we were poor and lived out on a farm away from everyone that we didn't get included in school and community activities. In my mind, it was just a natural result of our circumstances.

I didn't recognize the face of prejudice when my fourth-period algebra teacher gave me a dime each day and sent me off to Bill's service station to get a bottle of Coke for him while the class went on with their math lessons. Years later, however, that experience came back to me when I had to repeat Algebra 101 during my second year of college.

So then, my first year as a teenager, it was with a great deal of eagerness that my brother Jack and I took Uncle Wilford up on his offer to cut some cedar fence posts for him. The deal was that we could use his team and wagon and cut the posts on his land. In return, we could have every third post to sell for ourselves. We soon found a willing buyer and agreed to deliver fifty posts in ten days. The price set was twenty-five cents each. That would be twelve dollars and fifty cents. We began to dream of all the things we could do with our profits.

However, by noon of the first day on the job, reality set in. It was seven miles to the cutting site, and the heat from the early July sun hovered in the nineties. We had five posts on the wagon and an equal number of blisters on each hand from swinging the ax.

I've learned since that cedar posts are best cut in winter when the sap freezes and the heat generated by the work is countered by winter temperatures. During these times, a single blow from a sharp ax can sever a two-inch limb that would require three or four chops during the summer.

By nightfall, we had twenty-five posts on the wagon. Jack and I headed the team homeward and collapsed on the seat in total fatigue. We both dozed as the team retraced its steps to town and the barnyard. By the time the last post was unloaded and the horses were unharnessed and fed, it was late. We had earned two dollars—a dollar each.

We made the two-mile walk home in silence, too tired to waste energy on idle conversation.

I could tell that Mom had been worried about us, but she just went about feeding us a late but welcome supper of bottled deer hamburger with bread and gravy.

We repeated the process over the next five days, carefully selecting the trees to be cut to assure that we had quality posts. In the process, we learned that taking time out to sharpen the axes was important if we were to maintain our pace. It was a lesson—taking care of and maintaining tools—that has paid dividends ever since. We also learned that the horses, when asked to, could snap the last few inches of the tree trunk if we placed a chain at just the right location and height on the trimmed trunk, hooked it to the tugs, and then led the horses away. Thus, we developed a system that involved all available resources, which would lead us to think through future tasks and combine brains and brawn while completing them.

So it was with a great feeling of satisfaction that we loaded the last of our fifty posts onto the wagon for delivery. Having been given instructions regarding the location for unloading, we finished the task before noon and then took the team and wagon back to Uncle Wilford.

It was payday. We would buy a sack of flour for the family, get a sack of penny candy to share, and have enough left for a box of .22 bullets. The bullets were important. With them we could shoot magpies and turn them in for a bounty of five cents each. Magpie eggs were worth a penny.

It was late afternoon when the old farmer handed us five dollars and complained that the posts were too small. Even though I had been sent for Cokes by the math teacher, I still knew that five dollars was wrong and said so.

The farmer then gave us a lecture about minding our manners and said it was too bad our parents hadn't taught us respect. There was also some mumbling about too many Keisels and that with a father who came home only long enough to make another baby; it was "no wonder" we didn't know better.

"Ten cents each," he growed. "Take it or leave it!" And with that, he turned to leave.

Jack and I looked at each other, the anger and the empty, helpless feelings pushing tears to the surface and down our cheeks. We turned away from each other to hide the disappointment, wipe away the tears, and curse—first silently and then out loud.

"Damned if the old tightwad is going to get them for ten cents!" Jack yelled into the hands that covered his face to hide the tears.

For a long time, we sat in silence. There was no choice. We needed money for the sack of flour. With flour, Mom could bake bread and make gravy. There could be bread and milk, bread and gravy, and bread and butter, which came from the cream skimmed off the pans of milk from the daily milking of Stella, the family cow. With flour, there was a way to survive.

So we collected the five one-dollar bills that had been dug from the depths of the farmer's black pouch, which he kept in the chest pocket of his bib overalls. At least we could keep part of our promise to Mom. We would bring home the promised sack of flour and a couple of pounds of fresh ground beef. Mom could mix flour and eggs and an onion in with the meat and stretch a pound into the equivalent of two. We would eat well this night.

We'd brought the coaster wagon to town to haul the flour home in. On the way, we made plans to hunt magpies at night when they would be in their nests. We would locate the nests by day and return after dark, climb the tree or bush containing the nest, and capture the birds by hand. We would also harvest the eggs.

This method would not be as efficient as hunting in daylight, but since there was no money for .22 bullets, it would have to do.

When Mom was informed of the day's events, she told us that some people had no respect for their word but that she was proud we'd kept ours and delivered the posts as promised. There would, she said, be a day of reckoning for the farmer, who was known as Liberty Bell. "The name," she said, "is deserved because he's half-cracked." That was about the meanest thing we kids ever heard come out of her mouth. And it was a sign that she was with us.

The garden blossomed, and I got a job tromping hay and riding the derrick horse. My brothers Keith and Jack also got jobs. Things were looking up and the hard times had revealed lessons to be learned: When adversity strikes, first impressions can be critical. But, more often than not, it's the later impressions that matter most, shape the direction of our lives. My thirteenth summer was like that. Out of adversity came the hard-earned conviction that how we view life's journey is up to us-- that in adversity there can be hidden blessings, profound healing, acceptance, and understanding. It's an ill wind that blows no good.

The Incident

Beware of the law of unintended consequences.

THE ROAD OF life is marked by many signposts along the way. Weddings, birthdays, anniversaries, and such are markers just about everyone recognizes and celebrates. Other milestones, for all practical purposes, may go unnoticed by passersby.

Some may not have recognized the "Incident" as a milestone, but it was! This series of events would change how schools were designed in Sanpete County, the way girls dressed, and the nature of boy-girl relationships.

It was my thirteenth year and my seventh in school, and it was my first experience with physical education replacing recess. It was also a time to learn about showering, exercise, personal hygiene, and the gym. That was what the teachers taught. That was the official part of our education.

But there was another form of education to be had at the old gym, and almost every boy in the school enrolled in the "Class," which was all about girls. The "Classroom" was the result of some unique architecture that separated the boys' and girls' shower rooms with a double wall, with the plumbing in a two-foot-wide space between the two. The logic for this arrangement was obvious, and the logic that placed a small three-by-two-foot access door on the boys' side of the wall, creating the Classroom, was inspired.

As new seventh graders, we had a little curiosity about the door and what was on the other side, but it wasn't something to lose sleep over.

Anyway, the older boys weren't about to let seventh graders into the Classroom. That was reserved for ninth and tenth graders, who became resourceful and observant learners when the sound of running water and giggling girls filtered through the double walls.

Legend had it that a former class had found and duplicated the key to a previous lock. When that had been discovered, the lock got bigger, and the key became the sole property of the principal.

Puberty, however, is a relentless force, and this particular class of young men passing through their sophomore year was tormented by the taunting laughter and splashing water on the other side of the wall. Each day, it seemed, the sounds got louder. The situation became desperate when the senior boys, who now went to Snow High School, described in graphic detail the frolicking scenes from their days in the Classroom. The current male student body at the old school was viewed with disdain, even contempt, by the big boys when the subject came up.

Necessity, it is said, is the mother of invention, so a plan took form. The present lock would be cut and replaced with a look-alike. Secrecy was a must, so meetings were held between the big boys and every male student. It was made clear that anyone who failed to keep his silence not only would be denied admittance to the Classroom but also would thereafter be singing soprano as long as he lived. If he got to live at all.

The plan was to cut the lock with a hacksaw while the shower was full of boys. The fact that the door to the Classroom was in the far corner of the shower made shielding the work from view a simple task. Each class had a designated team: there were cutters, screen men, and lookouts.

A collection was organized to buy the new lock, and one's contribution to the fund would guarantee early access to the space between the walls. It was later reported that enough money had been raised to buy a hundred such locks. Nobody questioned the purchase committee; everyone just held tightly to their receipts verifying a contribution and hoped for early entry into the mysteries of the Classroom.

The sawing was painfully slow. Several hacksaw blades later, two-thirds of the lock still remained. While the character of the young men might have been in question, their persistence was not. At noon on the eleventh day, the word came down. The look-alike lock was in place, and Jake, by virtue of his worldly experience, had control of one key. "Spud" Thompson, the biggest, toughest bully in the school, had the other. They were keepers of the key and could have their way without challenge. They were gods among mere mortals!

One challenge remained: construction of the observation portals. The Classroom had room for three "observers," so three portals were mandatory. It was determined that the portals would have to be cut from the girls' side, where they could be positioned between the corners of the tiles. A drill with a quarter-inch steel bit would do the job, which would be carried out over the weekend in the dark of night.

Since the shower room was on the second floor, the windows were usually left slightly open to air the premises. The school's custodian, by chance, had left his stepladder along the wall below. Spud and two of his trusted lieutenants carried out the mission without a hitch.

Word that all was ready spread throughout the land. Spud, Jake, and Bull, another of the older boys, would be the first ones in the Classroom. Monday morning came, and the air was heavy with expectation. Small groups of boys gathered in the corners and recesses of the old school where passing girls were eyed with x-ray vision.

What happened next on that fateful day varies with the telling, but here's how time allegedly stood still from 10:45 to 11:00 a.m., according to one eyewitness account of what became known as the "Incident."

Some other students helped Spud, Jake, and Bull through the door and into the Classroom, and the door slammed closed behind them. Fifteen classmates stood at attention in anticipation. Shower water was changed from hot to cold, and beads of sweat broke out in moist palms.

Then, without warning, the Classroom door exploded open. Jake, overwhelmed by the enticing sights and unable to control himself, vaulted out, clad only in his best late-summer tan. His eyes were glazed and fixed, and his breathing came in rasping bursts, punctuated by caveman-like expressions of primeval origin. The cold water seemed to propel him onward through the crowded shower and into the locker room. There, at full speed, he snatched a towel from a classmate and disappeared through the dressing-room entry and onto the stage that separated the boys' and girls' changing rooms.

Tarzan would have cringed at the animallike screams that emanated from Jake's lungs. Some said the noise was akin to a bull elephant in full charge. Others likened it to that of a rutting bull elk. The charge carried him into the midst of the stunned girls, all in various stages of undress. The towel came up and lashed at the cheeks of screaming, fleeing young ladies.

One pass, two passes through the rows of lockers, and back across the stage he went.

The boys' locker room went deadly still for what seemed like an eternity; the only sounds were the heaving gasps for air coming from the bench where Jake sat, eyes riveted to the floor. Then, as if on cue, the other occupants exited en masse via any means available. Only Jake remained, resigned to whatever fate awaited him.

It was a black day. All the weeks of preparation simply evaporated. Jake, Spud, and Bull were expelled, banished. The doorway to the Classroom was bricked in. Girls' parents chased off anyone mentioned in connection with the "Incident." The school board investigated. Parents shadowed their children's movements like never before.

In new school buildings, the boys' and girls' shower rooms were placed on opposite sides of the gym floors. The girls now dressed in floor-length skirts with hoops inserted to keep them down. Big, bulky sweaters were the norm, and it was now impossible to tell what type of figure lurked beneath.

Not only that, but the boys' knowledge of the facts of life fell to an all-time low in my hometown. The bees didn't buzz, and the birds didn't sing.

Little did Jake, Spud, Bull, and the others know that the "Incident" would secure their place in the history of my hometown. What they'd done in those few Indian summer days was act out the rituals of life, dancing to the music of ancient physiological drives that placed a signpost along the road of life.

More Than Words

Life is full of consequences—for better or worse.

When I was a boy of ten or so, we lived on a small farm of twenty-five acres. We also worked another small farm on a sharecropping basis. It was there that I had my first personal encounter with tobacco.

On this particular day, wind, rain, and sleet were coming down with relentless fury. It wasn't supposed to be that way. It was springtime, mid-May, but it was also Utah.

Dad had charged my older brother and me with the first water turn, shepherding the spring ditchwater through long furrows. Shovels in hand, we found it to be a task requiring constant intervention. Cleaning debris from the ditch and furrows and clearing a path for the muddy water would make subsequent irrigation and the maturing of crops a practical outcome.

Soaked to the hide, I wanted to go home and leave the water to its own way. After all, the heavens were overflowing, watering the fields in wave after wave of sleet and rain. With each passing minute, my pleas to my older brother became more plaintive. But he was having none of it.

"Come with me," he ordered as he pointed to the corral at the head of the field. We took shelter in one of the sheds, but that didn't appease me. The cold wind was relentless, and I complained bitterly about it.

"I know how to warm you," my bother said as he fished out a package of cigarettes from the confines of the shed. "Here, take one of these and you'll get warmed up."

I took a puff or two, ready to try anything. It wasn't making me any warmer, though, and I said so.

"That's because you've got to get the smoke inside. Inhale it; suck it in," my brother advised.

Those would be the last words I'd hear for the next fifteen minutes. When the smoke hit my lungs, I forgot about being cold; I just wanted to purge myself of the demon that was upon me. Instinctively, I ran for water. No matter that it was the same muddy water that we were pouring down the furrows of the field. I puked, coughed, and gasped for breath while lying facedown in the mud at the ditch bank.

About that time, Mom drove up with coats for us. That brought a warning from my brother: "You tell, and you'll be sorry." I don't remember the ride home—or the next three or four days, for that matter. I think Mom knew, but she took pity on me.

As time went on, unintended consequences arose from that "warming experience." I couldn't be around anyone who smoked without having a physical reaction. I concluded that I was allergic to tobacco smoke. It was a mixed blessing, but one I now give thanks for.

Later on, I would be one of fourteen boys in my eighth-grade class. One of those boys was the son of our mayor. Mayor Larsen gave us a challenge: "None of you smoke or drink alcohol, and I'll buy your senior-class rings." It was game on, a challenge we took seriously.

All went well until a boy from another city moved to town and joined our class. Turns out he was smoker. We weren't about to let that cost us our reward, so a plan of action was set in place.

When a piano is out of tune, you fix it with a tune-up. Well, we had our own tuner-upper—a muscular kid with quick fists—and it transpired that the tuning session took place after school one day, out behind the baseball field's old grandstand.

We got our rings.

"Best tune-up I ever had," the boy-turned-man would say at a class reunion some fifty years later. Where there's a will, there *is* a way!

The mixed-blessing part of my introduction to smoking reared its ugly head one day several years later. I was in the army, having been drafted for the Korean War. The troop train I was on made a stop in El Paso, Texas, the home of Fort Bliss. I was continuing on, so I took advantage of the stop to stretch my legs and get a hamburger in the depot café.

Seated at a bar-like counter, I was eating my burger when a big, tough-looking first sergeant sat down next to me. He placed his order, asked where I was headed, and then lit up a big cigar. When he blew the smoke in my face, there was a spontaneous reaction. I barfed—all over the countertop, on his food, on him, and on the floor as I ran for the door. The timing of my escape couldn't have been better; my train was about to leave the station without me! Running hard, I jumped for and landed on the platform of the second-to-last car. I stayed out there, gulping fresh air, for a long time. If that sergeant hadn't blown smoke my way, I would have missed my train.

I was in my twenties at that time, and I remember feeling invincible. I was six four and 230 pounds of muscle and energy, but smoking was still my Achilles's heel. I've often wondered how that had come to be and why I've been afflicted/blessed in this way. But out of it all, I've concluded that the lesson I needed to learn was that the immediate consequences and impacts of my behavior are always more effective teachers than words.

Shoot-Out at the Old Barn

Discretion is the power to choose consequences.

In the 1930s and '40s, it wasn't unusual for one's extended family to live under the same roof. My family lived with my grandparents on my father's side until I was a fourth grader. Two uncles and one cousin, the daughter of an aunt, also lived in the home. A total of twelve people. Next door, an uncle and his family lived on the same lot.

We shared everything and wandered in and out of each other's houses as though we belonged. At mealtime it wasn't unusual to have a different set of people around the table at any given time, especially on weekends and during the summer when the kids were out of school.

We occupied half of a city block, about three acres, and everybody worked the land and cared for the livestock. We had big gardens, fruit orchards, and hay for the cows. There were pigs and chickens as well. We lived, in large part, off the land.

The livestock were housed in a large barn a short distance from Grandpa and Grandma Keisel's house. The barn had a loft over the pens below and, with its stacks of hay, was a favorite gathering place for the kids. There, we gathered to tell stories and make plans for the day. Sometimes we scheduled trips into the nearby foothills. Other times we spent an afternoon at the swimming hole in the creek that coursed through town.

We'd built a rock dam across the stream that flowed from the mountains above town. A rope hung from the branch of the big cottonwood along its bank. We performed all kinds of launches into the water from the rope, and cries that would make Tarzan proud erupted from the old swimming hole on hot summer days.

Late one afternoon, I was in the loft of the old barn with my older brother, Jack. We were hunting sparrows with our flippers, small handmade slingshots cut from willows. Both of us had a pocketful of small, round rocks that could be launched from the flipper with some degree of accuracy. When a sparrow flew into the barn, we took aim and fired. If we happened to knock the bird from its perch, the family cat quickly made off with its evening meal.

On this occasion, the birds were wary and fluttered in and out of the barn without landing. Jack and I were about to leave when Uncle Jake entered the barn below to do the evening milking of Stella, the family cow. Stella was a gentle old critter that gave us rides around the corral and the neighborhood. Sometimes we climbed on two or three at a time.

Uncle Jake washed the bag and teats and sat down on the stool to accomplish the task. At that moment, a light went on in my head. The flipper came up, the old rubber inner-tube bands were pulled back, and a pea-sized rock launched through the opening into the stable below. When the little rock struck old Stella in the ribs, she promptly went into a crow-hop in Jake's direction. This caused him some consternation, and he slapped Stella on the rump while admonishing her to "hold still, damn it!"

Well, the game was on! When Jack and I had regained our composure and cleared the tears of laughter from our eyes, Jack insisted, "My turn!" Same result. After a couple of turns each and an increasingly agitated response by cow and milker alike, we cut out the side entry to the street and disappeared into the gathering darkness.

At the supper table that night, Uncle Jake scratched his head in bewilderment as he told us about Stella's behavior at milking time. Grandpa Keisel said, "She probably has sore teats. Have you been using Vaseline?" Uncle Jake said he'd run out and then got chewed out for neglecting to get more. "You know better than that," Grandpa said. "Next time you might get your head kicked off! I'd kick, too, if you were pulling on my sore teats!"

Jack and I were the picture of sweet innocence. This was getting better all the time. A repeat performance was mandatory.

That night we slept out under the stars, as we often did on warm summer nights, which made it easy to slip into the barn as the sun peeked over the mountain to the east at dawn. A few minutes later, we were ready as Uncle Jake entered the stable below for the morning milking.

Since there had been no opportunity to obtain Vaseline, Uncle Jake washed the bag and teats and rubbed a generous coat of pine-gum salve on each of the four of them. He then put a set of hobbles on Stella. She looked around at him with big brown eyes, wondering what she'd done to deserve this shackling. Nevertheless, she stood quietly as the milking began.

After a respectful pause, we launched the first pebble, one just big enough to create a bit of irritation on Stella's thick hide. As before, Stella crow-hopped high in the air, switching her tail at the intruder. But because her hind legs were hobbled, she lost her balance and pinned Uncle Jake to the wall. She righted herself and sent the milk bucket in Uncle Jake's direction, its contents dousing the front of his bib overalls.

Such cussing as Stella received wasn't fit for man or beast. "What the hell's got into ya, ya old bitch?" Uncle Jake repeated again and again. There was also some other stuff we didn't understand about Stella's ancestry and her future if she didn't straighten up.

Well, things calmed down, but just for good measure, Uncle Jake tied old Stella to the manger. Jack and I debated whether another shot was wise, but in the end, the temptation was too great. We had to be careful now, since all the upheaval had changed the target's position. Instead of being on the far side of the cow, Uncle Jake was positioned at an angle that left him exposed.

Fighting to control my laughter, I loaded and pulled back the flipper. My aim had been good, but the tiny pellet, flying at dazzling speed, veered off to the right and, in less than a second, found a target just above Uncle Jake's left ear! He let out a bloodcurdling yell and toppled backward off the milk stool.

It was too much! Jack and I laughed out loud and were discovered. Uncle Jake got to his feet, held on to the manger while the cobwebs cleared, and then shouted, "You little bastards! You little bastards!"

That was enough for Jack. He made tracks out the side exit and headed up the street. I couldn't! I was weak with laughter, and my legs were like Jell-O. Uncle Jake had left the barn and gone to the house. I heard the kitchen door slam, and the cursing grew louder as he made his way back to the barn.

Suddenly I feared for my life. But still, my legs wouldn't go. Somehow I managed to roll out the side exit and stagger up the street. I'd gone only a few yards when I heard Uncle Jake behind me. That gave me a little boost, but the distance between the two of us was closing fast. My only chance was to get over the four-foot rock fence to my right.

I lunged at the wall, belly flopping across its top. At that moment, Uncle Jake caught up to me. He plucked the flipper from my back pocket and began shooting me on my exposed rear end. Again and again, he drew the rubber bands back to their maximum stretch and, like a drum, tattooed my backside. All the while, he was making wild statements about my ancestry—and his!

At the same time, Jack was hiding on the inside of the rock fence not far from me. Fearing for my life, he reached up and pulled me over the top. With that, somehow my legs came back, and we darted through the garden and into the safety of a grove of plum bushes. Out of sight, we slipped between the boards of the slab fence and headed for the nearby foothills.

It was sometime after dark before we made our way back home. Even then, we weren't ready to push our luck, so we showed up at Uncle Ken's supper table. Needless to say, the events of the day had already been shared with one and all. Word of our whereabouts reached home, and Dad came over.

We all had a good laugh, but Dad said, "Sooner or later I'm going to have to do something about you two. You could have really hurt somebody that way. You're lucky that rock only left a small welt on your Uncle

Jake's neck." With that, he paused and said, "Uncle Jake and Grandpa are going out to the sheep herd in the morning. I'll tell them I took care of things. In the meantime, no more!" We knew what he meant, but that night, just for safety's sake, we moved our sleeping-out beds into the shelter of the plum bushes and stayed there until midday to make sure Uncle Jake and Grandpa had gone off to the sheep herd.

I didn't show Mom and Dad the black-and-blue welts on my rear end. Discretion, I'd learned, was the better part of valor, as they say. After a week or so, the soreness faded from my backside, and I could ride old Stella at a gallop again. All was well.

Miss Phillips and the Wizard of Oz

If it's meant to be, it will find a way.

I HAVE BEEN fortunate in my lifetime to have crossed paths with some people who were quiet heroes. What they did was less important than who they were. Who they were was a product of many complex and subtle things, but the consistent threads of kindness and a general sensitivity were apparent. There was an appreciation for life and an overriding positive attitude.

Each of these individuals had developed a love, whether it be animals, music, or learning that gave them a strong center, determined who they were.

Lucy Phillips was that kind of person. I had seen Lucy on the streets of Ephraim and knew she was a school teacher. That's what she did. Little did I know that this woman with her classic "old maid" school teacher countenance would impact and determine, to a great extent, not only what I do but also who I am.

The first real contact with Lucy came when I found myself in her high-school English grammar class as a junior. Miss Phillips also taught English literature at Snow College. Back then Snow College was a small Utah junior college that enrolled high-school juniors and seniors as an integral part of the program. We were the freshmen and sophomores of the four-year offering.

I was startled when Miss Phillips, who always seemed to move in slow motion, looked squarely at me and said, "Mr. Keisel, I want to see you after school tonight." That was all. Nothing more!

The rest of that first class was a blur. Try as I might, I couldn't think of anything I had done that would require a trip to Miss Phillips's classroom after school—especially not on the very first day.

The event wasn't lost on my friends. "Glad I'm not in trouble," Cob Greaves said in his best concerned but mocking tone. Snar Jorgensen kept referring to my meeting with Miss Phillips as "a date with your new girlfriend, in fact your only girlfriend!" throughout the day.

Finally, it was time. I made my way downstairs and to the far end of the basement hall and Miss Phillips's room. She was there, behind her desk. Miss Phillips looked very old, her gray hair pulled back in a loose knot at the back of her head. Round spectacles tilting down on the end of her nose accented the wrinkled face that turned my way.

It was then that I saw the eyes! Miss Phillips looked straight at me, a slight smile creasing her mouth. In those first moments, I knew this teacher was more than the "old maid" image she portrayed outwardly in dress and physical appearance.

"Mr. Keisel,"—she always called me Mr. Keisel—"I have been looking at your records, and we have to do something about your grades!" All the time, Miss Phillips was drilling straight into my eyes with hers. When I looked away, she said, "Look at people when they talk to you! That'll help you remember what they say and will get their respect." It took years before the truth of that bit of wisdom surfaced in my contact with others, but the words ring true, having withstood a lifetime test.

"I know all about you and your family. I'm here to tell you that being poor and from the other side of the tracks is no excuse for those grades. When you earn grades like that, you just show the world that it's right; we can't expect a kid from a welfare family and an alcoholic father to amount to much!" she said in her quiet, matter-of-fact manner.

Before I could respond, she shoved a sheet of paper my way and informed me that beginning then we would "differentiate between what is *serious* and what *is trivial*."

The paper contained a quote from Frank Baum's *The Wizard of Oz*. I was told that in tomorrow's class she would call on me to read it out loud and to tell the class what it meant.

"If you need help after you have worked at it on your own, I'll be here before school starts tomorrow," she concluded. With that she went back to her papers.

Sheer panic hit me. I was like a cornered animal, but somehow I sensed this woman was real and that as she later told me, "If you go through life making excuses, you will become one. What you need to know is a sense of I can achieve."

What I didn't know then was that this teacher had used the same no-nonsense approach with two or three, however many there happened to be, boys every first day of school for the past twenty or so years. Her "boys" would become doctors, dentists, lawyers, scientists, and teachers. If anyone had told me I would become a teacher, I would have laughed at them in disbelief.

In fact, if anyone had told most of my teachers I would become a teacher, principal, and superintendent, there would have been a collective utterance of disbelief. Even now, some who have gone to a better place must turn over in their graves at the thought.

The next day I read the words from *The Wizard of Oz* and somehow managed an explanation of their meaning.

The quotation was just three sentences. "Brains are not the best thing in the world," said the Tin Woodsman.

"Have you any?" inquired the Scarecrow.

"No, my head is quite empty," answered the Tin Woodsman, "but once I had brains, and a heart also; so having tried them both, I should much rather have a heart...for brains do not make one happy, and happiness is the best thing in the world."

Off and on during the years that have followed, I have had occasion to reflect on the words' meaning. Without a general sensitivity and kindness, brains don't count for much I've concluded.

Miss Phillips had that sensitivity and kindness. Sometimes it came out in tough love where she called the shots. Sometimes she negotiated, but always she listened. Often teachers and others who don't listen well aren't aware that they don't. "Listening well helps us to excel in our own way and eliminates the need to make excuses," Miss Phillips would counsel her charges again and again. I've come to realize that what Miss Phillips did with the "Wizard Assignment" was to set me up for success. When I finished reading it and had shared my thoughts about its meaning with the class, Miss Phillips smiled and gave me a thumbs-up and exclaimed, "Well done!"

The conversation and assignments continued off and on over the next two years, and I graduated from high school with the possibility of college and a coaching career firmly implanted in my thoughts.

It would be nearly five years before I found myself back in Miss Phillips's classroom. Money for college would have to be something I took care of on my own, and the Korean War (it was called a police action) came along.

In retrospect it was a time of growing up, a time for experiencing life outside the sheltered valley of the Sanpitch. I spent my twentieth and twenty-first years in the army.

I earned eighty-five dollars a month for the first six months and had half of that sent home to help things out there. The US Army matched that, and even though I was on the other side of the world, I felt good knowing I was able to help at home.

That experience also brought the GI Bill and made it possible to come back to Snow. I made a point of looking up Miss Phillips and renewing old friendships.

Miss Phillips informed me that there was no excuse now and that she was there to help me if I needed it. She also planted a seed for contemplation when she suggested, "You really ought to have something more substantial than coaching. How about an English major and coaching minor?"

After that, I found myself enrolling in literature and writing classes but still had very real doubts about an English teaching major. Miss Phillips encouraged me to spend extra time in the language arts, but she also encouraged me to explore as many disciplines as I could while I had the chance. "The reason you explore is that now is the time of life to discover what you do best," she advised. "And always remember that even eagles walked before they flew. So don't give up on something too soon if it holds your interest."

By the end of my second and final year at Snow, I had determined that I would major in English and minor in coaching at Utah State University.

That spring, when I picked up my grades for the final term, there were two surprises. My grades were all As, a first for me, and a note from Miss Phillips was included. The message was simple: "You're on your way!"

Hand-Me-Downs

We should not be discouraged about
what is and what is not fashionable,
only mindful of what is or is not respectful.

Being the third of six boys in a family of fourteen children, I was the beneficiary of a steady flow of hand-me-downs. Hand-me-downs not only were passed down by my older brothers but also came from the closets of relatives, friends, and a widow in our neighborhood who had two boys about my size.

During World War II, there were a lot of shortages and rationing. People had financial issues, and we sure didn't know anything about designer jeans, Adidas shoes, or previously owned 501s with holes in the knees and other unmentionable places. Not that we didn't have holes in our Levis; we did. But Mom kept a watchful eye, and when the threads wore thin, a patch went on, and the jeans stayed in service. If we'd known how fashionable ragged Levis and jeans would become, we could have saved Mom a lot of work.

Similarly, when my brother went into the navy and left behind some too-big shirts and pants, I could have made use of them right away if I'd only known that I was a trendsetter—just fifty years ahead of my time. The pants would have hung on the lower extremities of my cheeks with the crotch at knee level, while the shirttails would act as a safety net in case there was fallout.

I did, however, take over the too-large cowboy boots—not to be fashionable, but because my own ankle-high shoes had given their all, successively, to each of three twelve-year-olds: my two older brothers and me.

The cowboy boots were several sizes too big, so I had to walk kind of stiff legged, my ankles locked and my toes pointing skyward. But they were my big brother's boots, and he was serving his country, so I was proud to wear them. I even tucked one pant leg inside, so my classmates and teachers could admire the design crafted on the leather uppers.

When the weather turned cold, my dad, older brother, and I set out a trap line for muskrat. We worked the Sanpitch River and the springs and ditches along its course. By early December, we made our first sale, and I got new shoes. The old boots went back under the bed, awaiting my brother's return from the war.

The trap line was good. A prime dark-glossy-brown pelt brought as much as a dollar and a half each. Once Leon "Slick" Stevens gave us two dollars each for a dozen extra-large pelts with fur that was long and thick from the cold January weather.

I took a dollar and a quarter from that windfall and negotiated the purchase of a baseball mitt from Leon Kelson. "Kels" even threw in a pair of modified baseball shoes. He'd taken an old pair of wing tips, removed the worn heels, and attached the cleats from a set of "real" baseball shoes with shingle nails. Because the shingle nails were too long and poked through inside, Kels had clinched them over and covered them with a piece of cardboard.

So it was that I proudly walked onto the field at the Ephraim team try-outs that spring. No one paid any attention to my hand-me-down cleats. I kept them polished for each Sunday afternoon game with some mutton tallow and a rag.

I got to play a little first base when the score was right, and I learned a lot about life as I listened to the big boys talk about girls, fishing, and the war.

At the end of the last game, Vance Allred, our team coach, motioned me over to his old pickup truck. "Keeze," he drawled, "what size shoe do you take?"

"'Bout eleven, eleven and a half," I responded.

With that, he dug into the sack of baseball bats and fished out a pair of Wilson cleats, tied together at the laces.

"I'm getting too damned old for this game," he said quietly. "Anyway, you take these, and remember, they're used to winning! That's why I want you to have them."

I choked out thanks and cut through the lot behind the grandstand. Halfway through, I slipped into the security of the plum bushes and took off my old hand-me-down wing tips. Setting them aside, I stuck my feet into the Wilsons and snugged down the laces.

The gift of the too big shoes and the thought that, in his eyes, I could be a winner gave me encouragement...something to build on in the days to come. I had some room to grow inside the Wilsons. They were size thirteen. No matter; I had a year to do it in, and I had a lifetime friend in the man who passed on those old hand-me-downs that warm Sunday afternoon.

Choices and Consequences

You are free to choose,
but you are not free from the
consequences of your choices.

THE SCRIPTURES TELL us that we will harvest that which we plant. If we plant wheat, we'll harvest wheat. It's the way things work. What applies to the plant and animal kingdom applies to us as well.

With us humans, it's about choices and consequences. These are the determinants of our harvest in the game of life. It's a simple law, one that is evident everywhere we look. And the conclusion is always the same: "As ye sow, so shall ye reap."

Still, for one reason or another, in our efforts to get what we *think* we need, we often choose to ignore the consequences part of the equation. The consequence, or the harvest of our choices, is in direct proportion to the energy we invest in the choice. For example, if one chooses to *be* a friend, one will *have* friends. Choosing not to be friendly will harvest unfriendly relationships with others. Words that lift others will come back to lift us.

When I made choices my dad didn't approve of, he used to put it like this: "If you're going to roll around in the muck with the pigs, you're going to come out smelling like one." It was his way of telling me that the consequences of certain choices were not good, but they were a sure bet if I persisted in making smelly choices.

While some would have us believe that we often don't have choices, there are, in fact, *always* choices. That's the reality of life; choices will always be available to us.

And whether we think so or not, every choice we make is sure to be witnessed by someone. Each Sunday when I meet an old friend at church, he asks the same question: "You been behaving yourself?" I always give the same response: "As long as anyone is looking."

To which he replies, "Well, you're OK then, 'cause you and the Lord are always looking." It's funny how that conversation limits the choices I have and gives me reassurance that even when "nobody's looking," someone always is.

A friend of mine shared an experience about choices and consequences. His grandson was living with him on his farm, where the alfalfa field was irrigated by a sprinkler system that required moving the pipes and sprinkler heads down the field by hand. When a section was suitably irrigated, the system was moved to the next section.

The grandson was "hired" to move the pipe. He would be paid when the field was irrigated. As all of us sometimes are, the boy became impatient and skipped a section or two along the way.

When the bottom section was finally soaked, the boy asked for his pay.

My friend, however, said, "Let's check your work."

They walked onto the field, where Grandpa kicked at the soil on the edge of the last section. It was moist and soft. The two then went to the next section, and the process was repeated. This time the soil was dry and hard.

"That's strange," the boy's grandpa exclaimed. "What do you think happened here?"

After a long silence, the boy dropped his head and whispered, "You know what happened."

Then an unexpected consequence befell the boy. "You're fired!" his grandpa exclaimed.

"What?" the boy questioned.

"You're fired!" came the response. "I can't afford to pay for a job half-done, and the cows can't eat hay that isn't there."

It was a hard lesson, but the boy's respect for his grandpa has grown with the passing years. He probably won't be leaving a job half-done in the future, as Grandpa has taught him a truth—that choices have consequences, and when we choose the behavior, we choose the consequences as well. Pick up one end of a stick, and you lift the other end, too.

The Wise Bench

A little laughter makes things work better,
last longer—especially relationships.

MORE THAN BEING the seat of judgment, if the Wise Bench could talk, what tales would it tell? Would it speak of love, laughter, sorrows, life, and simply give us the threads (stories) that weave the cloth of our own identities?

Coming out of the Great Depression and two brutal wars, any man in my hometown without a nickname meant he wasn't what the old-timers called "one of us." Without a nickname, a man was like a misplaced thread in the fabric of our community. Passed on from one generation to the next, nicknames told the story of the people like nothing else could.

In the beginning, there was "Perty" Pete, "Peephole" Soren, and "Alphabet" Aha. Those men and more have passed on, but the tradition of nicknames has not. I grew up with "Sad" and "Sorry" Anderson, brothers. Sad got that moniker because he never married, while Sorry was that way because he had. There was "Lagger" Green, a champion marble player, and Roy "Doughnuts." Roy was said to have a hole between his ears. Then there were the "Buck" brothers. It was said they would do most anything for a buck.

I've seen lists from the early days numbering well over two hundred nicknames. My brothers and I recently recited some seventy names from the '40s and '50s. Among them was "Liberty Bell"; it was said he was half-cracked.

There were a number of gathering places along Main Street in Ephraim, places where the town's menfolk gathered to spend some time relaxing, commenting on the day's news, and keeping track of the comings and goings of locals and strangers.

One of those places was the Wise Bench. The bench's designation, like the men's nicknames, was a tongue-in-cheek acknowledgment of the gossip and judgment that took place there. It was a place reserved for those who supposed they'd lived long enough to accumulate experience and seasoning worthy of a seat.

One day, a well-dressed stranger approached the occupants of the Wise Bench and asked, "Could one of you gentlemen tell me where I might find Vernon Olsen?" No one on the Wise Bench recognized the name. The stranger persisted. "No one knows Vernon Olsen? He lives, I'm told, on a farm just on the outskirts of town."

That's when Vern "Tooley Hoot," one of the men on the bench that day, suddenly stood up, looked the stranger in the eye, and declared, "Hell, that's me! What da ya want?"

The fact that few women earned nicknames was probably due to respect, among other things. Still, there *were* some women who joined the men in the ranks of nickname identity—the "Black Widow," for example. A woman with distinctive long black hair—she'd had three husbands, all of whom had died shortly after marrying her.

As with most nicknames, if you missed the tongue-in-cheek innuendo attached to the name, then that wasn't all you were missing. After all, it's the little things, the ordinary turned *extra*ordinary through a nickname, that give flavor and substance to the journey of life. Like *The Book of Knowledge,* a man who thought he knew everything said, "You know you've struck it rich when you have silver in your hair, gold in your mouth, lead in your behind, and a nickname."

So, how did the tradition of assigning nicknames take root? Maybe it was because these names conveyed simple truths. More than likely the practice had to do with making hard times a bit softer—not letting the fires of life remove the ability to laugh at ourselves and each other. A very real possibility is that the names just fit a particular personality or occasion.

For example, "Sawdust" ran a sawmill. "Minute Man" was so punctual you could set your clock on his comings and goings. "Tut-Tut" stuttered when he got excited. There was "Big Dick" and "Little Dick," the tall and short of it. The "Cattle Baron" had about forty cows. Finally, there was "Joe Mormon Preacher." Enough said.

Looking back, I see now what I didn't see then. For some, a seat on the Wise Bench was food for the soul. It was there, seated at the bench, that the lonely could find acceptance, fit in, laugh again, and push aside the realities of everyday life. There, too, the culture of nicknames sometimes allowed men to reject society's sense of what should be proper and just be themselves. Never meanspirited, the talk and the nicknames tended to soften the realities of everyday challenges and provide a sense of belonging.

That medicine—belonging and laughing at life—can make all of us, like the Wise Bench regulars, forget ourselves. It did then. It still does today. If the Wise Bench could talk, oh, the tales it could tell.

Lessons in the Rearview Mirror

Life begins the day we decide to live it.

There were two school experiences in my life that had vastly different outcomes with respect to my image of myself. Both events were negative in nature, both came my way at the hands of teachers, and both occurred at a time when impressions were a vital force in shaping my view of what I could or could not achieve—that is, how I would live my life.

The first one occurred in eighth grade. Posters went up announcing tryouts for the upcoming school production of *Duel in the Sun*. A friend, a girl I hung around with during the school day when the boys weren't there, asked if I was trying out.

Until that moment, I'd never let such a thought even enter the backroads of my mind.

"Nah," I replied. "I wouldn't know how to do that."

My friend mentioned something about helping me rehearse and prepare, saying, "It would be fun to do this together." She gave me a little smile and batted her eyelids a time or two before heading off down the hall. I think it was then that I noticed girls were built different from boys.

The next day, my friend handed me an audition sign-up sheet and suggested that since she was going to try out for the lead, it would be "neat" if I tried out for the Gary Cooper role. I'd seen the movie, and everything about Cooper's performance shouted, "Hero, hero, hero!"

Well, needless to say, as I watched her walk down the hall again, truly confirming that girls *were* different from boys, I decided to take the bait. Like a hungry carp, I rose to the surface and inhaled—hook, line, and sinker!

That afternoon, when school was out and the halls were empty, I dropped my completed audition form on Miss Mansfield's desk. That in itself was an act of bravery. Miss Mansfield, it was said, could kill a fly at forty yards with a single glance. I'd never seen the corners of her mouth turned any way but down.

As I hastened to exit her presence, she stopped me in my tracks, saying, "Your audition is right after school tomorrow." So much for practicing with my leading lady. Nonetheless, I was determined to go through with it. After all, I'd survived submitting my audition form to Miss Mansfield.

The audition consisted of saying a few lines and singing one of the show's songs, and I was allowed to try out using the song sheet. That was like a life jacket that was too small, but it was better than nothing. However, as I found out, it wasn't enough to do the job.

One thing about the audition experience is embedded in my mind like a hot branding iron on the flank of a young steer. I'd completed the dialogue and managed to get through the song, and I stepped offstage, out of sight. But there I overheard a conversation between Miss Mansfield and two other teachers who were overseeing the auditions.

"Well, what do you think?" one of the teachers asked.

"Sounds like a jackass in pain," came the reply from Miss Mansfield.

There were muffled laughs and then a loud snicker as Miss Mansfield continued, "So much for that. Let's get on with the real tryouts." My confidence and self-esteem shattered by the words; I slipped away.

The second experience occurred a year later when I was assigned to an algebra class. As the class got under way on the first day and the teacher gave students some class time to work on the day's assignment, he came by my desk and handed me a dime.

"Run downtown and get me a cold Coke," he ordered. I looked at him in surprise, at which he said, "You won't need this stuff anyway. It's just for kids who are going to college." Another hot branding iron.

At the time, college wasn't part of my vision of the future. That would come later at the hands of another teacher.

Each day for the rest of the year, I was given a dime and made the journey to Bill Nielson's service station for the Coke. Needless to say, I learned no algebra that year. My report card said I did C– work. It lied!

Both of these experiences left their mark. No, I do not raise my voice in song, but I *have* been successful in meeting the mathematics requirements for graduate degrees.

The first experience stopped me cold in my tracks like a court sentence with no appeal. The second served as motivation to lift myself up, to prove that I was college material.

In the case of math, I stopped driving through the rearview mirror of life. That image said, "You won't need this stuff (you're not capable of this stuff, poor trash); it's just for kids who are going to college!"

On the other hand, when there's singing to be done, I'm locked into my rearview-mirror image and the braying jackass reflected there. My life is thus less than it might be if I could only go beyond the images of that day long ago.

Traveling life's roads through the rearview mirror is like that. It's only when we see that life has two mirrors that we're able to move beyond the singular, one-dimensional reflections of our rearview-mirror image.

Been There, Done That

To live a fulfilling life, play a little each day.

When my kids and grandkids ask what I did for fun when I was growing up, I answer, "We made our own entertainment. No cell phones, iPads, video games—just us and our imagination."

In my younger years, fun might have involved something as simple as playing hide-and-seek, a game of marbles, or a card game called Go Fish. For my brothers and me, hunting sparrows with a flipper was on the menu. We could spend hours shooting small rocks at cans lined up on the fence.

We had a milk cow named Stella. We also had a saddle, so it seemed natural that the two would go together. Stella, gentle soul that she was, didn't take kindly to our riding double. Neither did Grandpa Keisel when he noticed a drop in milk production.

That left us with Margie, a big blue roan horse. She carried us around town, one or two at a time, during the summer. But winter changed all that. When the snow got deep enough, we attached one end of a rope to the saddle horn and the other to the handle of an old car-trunk lid. It made a great sled of sorts and could accommodate however many kids could pile on. Sad to say, that too came to an end when the owner of a rock fence, a cranky old woman who didn't like kids, complained that we went around the corner of her fence so fast that we knocked the rocks off the top of it.

Sleeping outside was fun as well. All it took was a couple of big patchwork quilts. Having a package of marshmallows and a fire in half of a fifty-gallon barrel was a bonus. Night games and spooky stories with someone out there in the dark making appropriate sound effects made us want to stay together, close to the fire's light and warmth.

As we grew older, my brothers and I expanded our activities to include authority figures in town. One of them, Hespert, was our town marshal. Like everyone else, he had one or two nicknames. "Despert" Hespert had a certain rhyme to it, but this belied his easygoing nature. So did his other moniker, the "Iron Claw." Despert Hespert was, in reality, a mix of Andy and Barney from *The Andy Griffith Show*. Just like in that episode where Otis, having had too much to drink, was left in an unlocked cell to sleep it off, Despert often left the jail cells unlocked so those imbibing too many spirits could go home or to work once they'd slept it off.

One of our favorite pranks with Despert and select teachers was to load the ends of their cars' tailpipes with potatoes, shoving them in tight to shut off the exhaust. When that happened, pressure from the running motor would build up until certain events transpired. The first was a loud engine backfire or two. The backfires inspired an immediate reaction from drivers and other occupants of the car as the potatoes exploded from the pipes.

One winter night, as was his habit, Despert sat in his car, a 1930s-something Ford sedan, with the motor idling to provide heat. It wasn't unusual for Despert to catch a few winks in the warm car. And so it was that when we saw his chin fall to his chest, a potato was shoved into the car's tailpipe. From the shelter of some bushes across the street, we watched with high expectations.

We weren't disappointed. When the backfire came, sounding like a gunshot, Despert's arms shot up over his head. The engine raced as he ducked down on the seat, hitting the accelerator in the rush. After a bit, the top of his head could be seen as he peeked about. Then, seemingly satisfied that nobody was close by, Despert exited the car on the curbside and hustled into the city building where his office was. His office window faced the street, but the light didn't come on, so we slipped away into the darkness.

After a suitable wait—it took several days for Despert to return to his habit of sitting and dozing in his car—we were back at it again. This time, however, the outcome was kind of disappointing. When the backfire came, Despert just shoved the car into gear and sped off.

At that, we had an inspiration! *Wouldn't it be fun to see what happened if Despert's back bumper was chained to the light pole at the curb's edge?* Before long, a solid plan took shape. Not wanting to tie the potato-in-the-exhaust-pipe prank in with the new plan, we determined that a noisy, late-night, speeding pass-by would trigger a chase. We could get away if the plan worked.

Not long afterward, an opportunity presented itself, and we went whooping and hollering past the chained-to-the-light-pole car. As anticipated, Despert's headlights and driver's-side red spotlight came on, but there was no chase. The chain had done its job.

We went out of town, circled around the valley, and then ventured quietly back through Main Street. This time there *was* a chase, but we had a good lead before the red light came on. That chase took us to the fields and the backroads that led to farmyards and hiding places. One by one, with the exception of the driver, we exited the car, went into hiding, and then walked home.

When it was my turn, Despert was hot on our heels. All I could do was jump the wire fence and hunker down in the tall grass and sagebrush that grew there. Screeching to a halt, the Long Arm of the Law, Despert Hespert, jumped out of his car, flashlight in hand.

"I know who you are!" he bellowed. "Come out with your hands up and nobody gets hurt," he repeated again and again. Since his light kept sweeping back and forth over the eighteen-inch-high alfalfa, I held my breath and hugged the ground.

After more yelling, cussing, and threats like "I'll lock you little #@$ &%$#s up and throw the key away," I heard him say something about headlights and then speed away. While he never caught any of us that night, it turns out that he suspected our identities and had a conversation with our parents. It was enough. We turned our energies to other pursuits.

Mysteriously, our history teacher, a guy of short stature with "Little Man Syndrome," found his outhouse hoisted to the top of his barn by way of the rail-and-cable system used to put hay in the loft.

Not long after that, when the principal turned the key to start his car, a gadget that released a plume of smoke and made loud whistling sounds under the car's hood was activated. Another teacher drove a Henry J, the forerunner of today's minicars. Two or three students could easily lift the rear of the car off the ground. Oil cans with an inch-thick board laid on top and placed under each rear spring shackle would raise the rear tires just a half inch off the ground.

When the teacher's several attempts to go forward and backward, gunning the engine and rocking back and forth in the seat while shifting gears, came to no avail, several of the "in-the-know onlookers" offered a push. The teacher, however, had decided that a tow truck was in order, so we went to the third-floor window to watch. The quandary was solved when the tow-truck driver discovered the cans while preparing to tow.

They say mum's the word, so life went on. Turns out our offer to push the car was a good move. We never did tell anyone that we'd planned to lift the car off the cans and then drop it when the teacher gunned the engine. Sometimes the good Lord looks out for us. That's not to say we totally abandoned the idea—we didn't—but the timing and place were wrong, so why tempt fate?

It was after graduating from high school that another driver and his Henry J would revive old memories. This time the driver was Ike; his given name was Isaac, but "Ike" sure sounded a lot cooler in the eyes of the eighteen-year-old boys who gathered at Frank's service station evenings and sometimes Saturday afternoons.

Ike was small of stature, maybe five feet tall if you stretched the truth. He probably didn't tip the scales at much more than a hundred pounds. He was a sheepherder who came to town for a month in the fall and spring to hang out in the Tyro Club and have a few beers. Ike liked to park his Henry J behind Frank's service station and then walk around the corner to the club.

Sometimes the return trip was on unsteady legs—too much beer. Seeing this pattern, we deemed it only logical that something should be done to create a bit of excitement. After all, the oil cans were right there. The Henry J was there. The muscle to lift the car was there, too.

One other factor made this a setup to order. Ike liked to back the Henry J within five feet of a fence, parking to one side of a gate. It all had a certain attraction, a call to action. Three of us would lift the Henry J while a fourth placed the cans and board platform beneath the rear spring shackles on both sides.

Having accomplished this, we retreated to Frank's to watch for Ike's approach from across the street. Seeing him round the corner, we ran to the gate behind his car and hid behind the fence there. Peeking out from between the fence boards, we watched as Ike got in, started the engine, and then released the clutch. Nothing happened. He shifted into reverse and got the same results. That procedure repeated itself several times before Ike got out, looked under the hood, and then got back in and started the process all over again. This time when he shifted out of reverse, he also hit the accelerator pedal hard.

That was our call to action. Jumping through the gate, we hoisted the Henry J up and pushed it forward, dropping it to the ground, its tires spinning and throwing gravel as Ike sped off toward the street. Frank and a couple of others watching from the station reported that Ike, wide-eyed, was thrust back into his seat but managed to navigate a quick trip around the station before coming to an abrupt stop. Getting out, he lifted the hood, stood back and looked around, and then carefully drove away.

A few days later, Ike came into the service station. "How's it going, Ike?" I asked. Pushing up close, raising his barely five-foot frame up on tiptoe, Ike locked eyes with me and declared, "Me follow you!"

"OK, Ike," I responded, "that'll be good."

"Me follow you," I learned, was Ike's way of saying, "I'm going to join you guys." And he did. During those visits, Ike joked about taking his Henry J to the salt flats where world land-speed records were set. It was a subtle reminder that he knew what we had done. He also shared stories of his life as a sheepherder and, on occasion, bought us a Coke. Needless to say, Ike's response to what we thought was a practical joke opened my eyes and brought a sense of respect where there had been little. Ike didn't change, but he changed us as we came to know him.

Later, when I became a school principal, students who were caught pulling a little mischief often asked, "How did you know?"

My response was always an honest: "Been there, done that!" Ike and others in my life's journey had left me with a simple truth: it's not where we've been or the things we've done that will determine who we are at the end of the day. Where we're going will. That's because all of us are works in progress.

A good friend, who changed the course of his life to become his town's marshal, put it this way: While sitting behind the wheel of his police car, he declared, "I've ridden in the back as well as the front seat. The view up here is way better."

Scrounging

Let the first helping hand we seek be at the end of our own arm.

THE ART OF scrounging hasn't been given its just due. I'm talking about scrounging to meet one's needs in the best traditions of work and honesty. Scroungers are innovators who acquire whatever they need from whatever source is available. To a scrounger, there's always more than one way to skin a cat. If necessity is the mother of invention, then scroungers are the fathers. They always find a way!

Scrounging takes a lot of energy, both physical and mental. A real scrounger isn't lazy and usually engages in several endeavors simultaneously. He's always thinking, always acting on his thoughts.

Failure doesn't discourage scroungers. If something doesn't work, they'll go at it from a new and different perspective.

Scroungers have become some of the world's most successful people. People like Ben Franklin and Henry Ford had to be scroungers. Not to mention General Patton and the Wright brothers.

A lot of scroungers, however, pass through life unknown by the world at large. My family was like that. With fourteen children and meager resources, exploring every possible means of support was important. Like the early settlers of this land, we and others like us learned to live off the land. We took only what we needed and left ample resources for sustaining a continuing supply.

Scrounging may have been easier fifty years ago. Life seemed simpler then. There weren't as many people, and the world we lived in was smaller. Many of us had grandparents who lived and died in the same house, and in the same town, as their own parents and grandparents. Today, however, the movement from a manufacturing society to an information culture has changed the nature of scrounging.

When I was a teenager growing up in Sanpete County in central Utah, I learned to scrounge for my wants and needs. I wasn't concerned about name-brand jeans and designer shirts—or a certain kind of sneaker. We didn't know about Pac-Man or the Sony Walkman. McDonald's, Burger King, and Kmart weren't inundating us with all their clever messages to compel us to buy their products.

And while parents wanted their kids to have more than they had, it seems they concentrated more on teaching them to *earn* their rewards instead of just handing things over. The result was a generation of scroungers who paved the way for innovative problem-solving and decision-making strategies that made the technology explosion of the '80s and '90s possible.

One of my earliest experiences in the world of scrounging was gathering Fisher Beer and Coke bottles. Back then, each bottle turned in at stores and businesses that sold these products would earn a kid like me a penny. On a good Saturday, I could make the fifteen cents necessary to buy a movie ticket and have a dime left over for popcorn and a candy bar.

When a farmer came by, heading south on Old Highway 89, I would hop on his horse-drawn wagon and ride along for two or three miles. I'd then walk back to town gathering any bottles I could find, hauling them in a gunnysack slung over my shoulder.

It was seven miles from Ephraim to Manti. We soon learned that most of the bottles were discarded one to two miles out, so we ventured beyond that only occasionally, when sufficient time had elapsed between trips to make it worthwhile.

One of my best sources was an old bachelor neighbor who lived in a one-room cabin a half mile to the north. We called him Jim Chinaman. I don't think he had any Chinese ancestry, but he was small of stature and had some Asian features, so "Jim Chinaman" it was. He used to consume a dozen or so bottles of Fisher Beer every couple of days.

Jimmy wasn't the best of housekeepers, so when we visited his garbage barrel and the customary number of bottles was absent, it meant a knock on the door and a visit inside. Jimmy wasn't always a cordial host, but he usually instructed us to help ourselves. We could peek through the small window and tell if it was safe to knock. If Mutt, Jimmy's loyal hound, was on the bed, not under it, it was OK to knock. Under the bed—better to come back another time.

In early spring when the magpies were nesting, their eggs provided a bounty of a penny each. The bird itself brought a nickel. I'm not sure who paid the bounty, but a weekend in the field could bring us a dollar or two. I don't think we hurt the magpie population, but I do think we drove some unsuspecting customers away from Spence Olsen's service station when the wind was just right. Five-gallon buckets of eggs and birds had an odor all its own.

Later, when I was a senior in high school, I ran a muskrat trap line from late November through February. I'd walk the line a couple of times a week and had traps on the flowing wells and ditches running from them to the Sanpitch River. The trap line then coursed south a couple of miles along the river's banks.

When I caught a muskrat, it took me only a minute or two to remove the hide, wash it, and reset the trap. I carried a small bag with the necessary equipment to maintain the line and transport the thick, rich brown fur home.

By the end of February, I took my season's catch to town and got price quotes from two hide buyers. The furs, depending on their size, brought from one to two dollars each. I had a payday of just under $400.

A battleship-gray 1941 Ford two-door coupe caught my eye. After some hard negotiations, I was able to buy my first car. It cost $275. I suddenly had some new friends.

Gas was nineteen cents a gallon, so I had to limit my driving. However, there were several gasoline distributors in town whose storage tanks were located alongside the railroad tracks on the west side of town where gas was delivered by rail. I soon discovered that the large hoses used to transfer gas from the railroad cars to the storage tanks were left with a gallon or so of fuel still in them after each use.

So, off and on for the next year, I would stop by and drain the hoses. One time, the son of one of the distributors discovered me in action. He'd come there for the same reason. I told him I wouldn't tell if he'd let me have the gas on Mondays and Fridays. It was a gentleman's agreement between scroungers.

We're not the same people today that we once were, but scrounging still has its place. We call its practitioners *entrepreneurs* today, but many of the conveniences we enjoy, those that have helped us and changed us, had their birth in the minds of scroungers. They are the driving force behind much of our traditions and culture.

Sometimes I worry about the future because we don't seem to have many "true" scroungers left. Then I look around and say, "I'm here. I'm doing it." And I know others are also scrounging. It's good to know somebody will always be around to carry on that wisdom and that knowledge.

A Lesson in Accountability

Life extends no free rides.

DURING MY YOUTH, going to school meant walking to and from school. This resulted in a daily journey of two and a half miles—rain, snow, or sunshine.

For the most part, my brothers and sisters and I enjoyed the experience. In the fall, plum bushes along the way provided after-school snacks. And, we could accumulate enough pop and beer bottles from along the roadside to buy us an occasional candy treat with the refund. It was also a time to visit with other kids who lived along the way.

Back then, we got to school on our own. Parents didn't have money for gas, even though it was less than twenty cents a gallon. School-bus service did not exist; everybody walked.

When I made the basketball team, Coach Mickelsen told those of us who lived a mile or more from school that we could skip conditioning laps after practice if we would run to and from school each day.

That created a problem in the morning, though, when I'd arrive at school soaked in sweat. We didn't have jogging sweats in those days, and our running shoes were the ones we had on our feet every day. The canvas gym shoes didn't do very well in snow.

In the beginning, everything was OK at home with the running. But before long, Mom didn't like the extra laundry the sweaty run produced, and then one of my friends demanded, "When was the last time you took a bath?"

One morning, as I left the yard a little late, the answer to my problem came down the highway from the south, heading toward town. Henry Pederson had moved his milk cows to his new corrals just a quarter mile from our place, and now, just like clockwork, he was delivering the milk to town.

As Henry pulled up alongside me, he yelled, "Jump in!" That wasn't much of a challenge, since Henry traveled in a spoke-wheeled Star. It was a 1920s-something vintage cruiser that ambled along at less than ten miles per hour. I arrived at school just as the first bell sounded, and I hadn't even broken a sweat.

That scenario repeated itself over the next ten days, and I was feeling good. No stinky remarks at school, and my running had been reduced to one way only. It was reduced, that is, until Mom caught on to the fact that I wasn't leaving along with the rest of the kids in the morning.

When she questioned me, my response was, "I run, so I don't need to leave when they do." Dad overheard the conversation and stated, "If you want to change your story, I'll let you tell it."

He went on, "I happen to know how you've been getting to school the last week or so." After that was cleared up, and I confessed that I'd promised Coach Mickelsen to run both ways, I took off for school, thinking all that was behind me. I should have known better.

That night, when it came time to run after-practice conditioning laps, I started to leave as usual. That was when the coach called me aside. "I understand," he said, "that you owe the team some conditioning work." Before I could confirm or deny the allegation, he continued, "Your mom dropped by earlier, so let's skip whether you do or don't owe them and find a way to correct the problem."

"I won't do it anymore," I responded.

"I'm sure you won't," he shot back, "but that still doesn't make up for the two weeks you cut out on us."

"I'll tell you what," he went on. "You run laps with the team, then run to and from school for the rest of the season too, and we'll call it even."

Since we were only a month into the season, it didn't take me long to figure out that I was paying back with interest. On the other hand, though, I became a much better-conditioned athlete, and my play improved as a result.

I also learned a lesson about accountability and the cost of trying to bypass a responsibility, a trust. The experience burned into my conscience the fact that even though I was getting older and thought I should be making my own decisions, I could not escape the consequences of violating my parents' and Coach Mickelsen's expectations.

The fact that my integrity wasn't conditional on whether outsiders discovered the transgression was made clear when Coach Mickelsen told me, "Keeze, you're lucky you have parents who care enough about you to hold your feet to the fire. Your mom could have cheated you by letting the thing slide. It must have been hard on her pride, but she put that aside and revealed what was going on because she knew it wasn't right."

As the winter snow grew deeper, Henry's chores took a little longer to complete. As a result, I could count on our paths crossing in front of J. T. Jackson's old place as he headed home in the dark.

The headlights on the Star were like a coal-oil lamp, giving off more of a sense of security than of light for any practical purpose.

Like just about everyone else in the valley, Henry had a nickname. His comings and goings were rituals that you could set your clock by. It seemed only natural that because Henry—like those patriots of the American Revolution who pledged to take the field at a moment's notice—was always ready, always accountable, always at the appointed place and time when he said he would be, he should be dubbed "Minute Man."

As boys will do, my brothers and I were often looking for ways to create a little diversity in life on the farm. Minute Man gave us that opportunity one Sunday evening when he left the Star parked just off the highway and walked through the deep snow to his corral a few hundred yards from the highway.

The old car had two-inch-wide tires mounted on wooden-spoked wheels. It took only a few seconds under the cover of winter's early darkness to pack a mound of snow around and through the spokes and wheels where they met the ground. The addition of a little water to the mix soon created an ice anchor at each of the four wheels.

Hiding in the safety of the high brush that lined the fence marking the highway right-of-way, we watched as Minute Man cranked the old horseless carriage to life. With the engine at idling speed, Minute Man stuck the gear in reverse and revved up the engine as he let the clutch out.

There was a crunch as the driveline strained to turn, and then the engine went silent. Henry said something rude about the car's ancestry as he climbed out and spun the crank, bringing the engine to life again.

This time when the clutch was released, the engine was at near full speed. The old Star shuddered and lurched backward. As the four ice-laden wheels rotated back, there was a loud crunching, grating sound as the ice blocks encountered the fenders. At that, Minute Man shifted to neutral and climbed down to inspect. All he found were a few chunks of frozen snow and ice, so he got back in and headed off down the highway.

It was a disappointed group of boys who watched Henry as he guided the big team of horses pulling the V-shaped snow plow up the lane to his corral the next day. We had won, and we had lost. It was over before it had really begun.

I guess Minute Man really had the last laugh. After that, he never offered me a ride again—just smiled, waved, and drove on by. Each time that happened, a small voice inside me asked, "Does he know?" Then just a tinge of guilt surfaced. But only for a second! Sometimes the consequence is worth the risk. Either way, there's always learning to be done when we make choices.

Rich Little Poor Boys

If you would be rich, do what you should,
not what you could.

Over the years, from time to time I've had conversations with my brothers about dreams and goals. When you grow up in poverty, a natural consequence is to dream about being rich. Maybe you dream about finding a gold mine or learning that an unknown rich relative died and left you a fortune. Not many people get rich that way. Most of us have a better chance of acquiring riches in nonmaterialistic ways.

Because of this, when my family reflects on our treasures, we don't dwell on how many dollars we've accumulated or what fancy cars and homes we might have acquired. What we've inherited is much more valuable. In fact, unlike some people I know, we can take our inheritance with us.

Mom used to tell us, "We're not poor; we just don't happen to have money." Even then, that message wasn't wasted on the seemingly deaf ears of children.

Nonetheless, for a family of fourteen children and their parents, being economically poor was a "hard row to hoe" in a society that valued material wealth and the social status that could come with it. The world has always been filled with the haves and the have-nots. I learned by my mother's example that how you viewed these two groups made all the difference. Her "we are not poor; we just don't have any money" attitude enabled her to walk in the company of the wealthy as well as the downtrodden with her head held high. She always offered a full measure of honesty and integrity to everyone, regardless of their station in life.

One time, Mom went into the Bank of Ephraim to pay a debt. Even though doing so would leave us penniless, she paid it. As she was leaving the bank, she noticed a twenty-dollar bill on the bank floor. Without hesitation, she picked it up and turned it in to the bank teller.

Later that day, Mom was telling us about finding the money. One of my brothers asked if he could have some of the twenty dollars to buy a box of .22 bullets that he would use to hunt magpies, which could then be turned in for a bounty payment of five cents each.

Mom's reply was, "I don't have it. I turned it in to the bank."

When asked why, she simply said, "It wasn't mine."

My brother responded, "We need it worse than the bank! They have plenty of money."

To that, Mom replied, "You're right, we do need it worse than they do, but we need our self-respect even more. You can buy a lot of things with self-respect, things money can't buy. Self-respect and honesty are concrete things; you know if you have them or not. After all, the most important things come down to what you do every day. When you forget that, that's when you run into trouble."

That "money found" experience has been burned deep inside my family's identity. It has fueled a driving passion to overcome hardship. For a time, my brothers and I labored under the impression that we had to lift ourselves out of economic poverty to show the "blue-nosed, high-society" faction that we were as good as they were.

Mom never took that approach, and the older we got, the more we learned by her example that sometimes people had a lot of money but not a lot of direction in their lives beyond making more. We also learned that winners don't sit around waiting for miracles. Victory comes to those who work the hardest and persevere to the end with their integrity intact.

"What enjoyment," she said about finding that money, "could I have in knowing the money wasn't mine?" It was a twenty-dollar experience that taught a priceless lesson. Wealth does not lie in possessing material riches but in living life with one's integrity intact.

Lessons of the Old Tree

When the fires of life rage, He always sends the rain.

I AM A member of the Church of Jesus Christ of Latter-Day Saints. I attend meetings most Sundays and have a couple of assignments, or callings, in my ward. Today I would probably be labeled "active" in church terms.

That hasn't always been the category I've fallen into, though. There have been times when I've felt removed from the church as a result of choices I've made and the intolerance of some who parade their status with pride, as in "I am among the chosen few, and you are not." Judgments are always black and white for these churchgoers on Sunday, but perhaps a little gray creeps in during the week.

When I've been pulled back to active status, it's been through the messages and actions of those who walk the talk—day in, day out. And while this group has included Sunday school teachers, bishops, and stake presidents (church leaders), many of my mentors are not active members in the sense that they pay their tithes, mark the rolls, and accept the church's callings.

Much of what I value—family, honesty, hard work, and respect for others—is rooted in the principles of the church. Many of the experiences and teaching moments reinforcing those values, however, were inspired by individuals whose names might have been absent from or labeled "inactive" on the rolls of the church.

I think there were a lot of those people in my hometown. They might not have made an appearance at our church on Sundays, but they did show up if someone needed a helping hand. You could tell by the way they treated people and animals that they had cut their own deal with their Maker and their own soul.

One of those individuals was Paul Hansen. Paul was a big, tobacco-chewing, bespectacled giant of a man who walked with a little hitch in his stride. I had the opportunity to work with and learn from Paul over several summers while working as a seasonal employee of the US Forest Service.

Paul could cuss with the best of them, but it was never meanspirited. The cussing always came with a glint in his eye and just a hint of a smile. Just the same, you perked up your ears when the cussing started. Yes, Paul would swear on occasion, but I never heard him lie. He took a glass of beer now and then, but he never thought of stealing or cheating, as far as I could tell.

One afternoon we were doing some trail work, and a thunderstorm rolled over the top of the ridge above us and down the canyon, where we took shelter beneath a big pine tree.

For a long time, we just sat in silence and watched the rain bounce off the trees and underbrush. A loud clap of thunder followed the crack and roar of a lightning bolt targeting a big old snag of a once-majestic pine tree standing on the brink of the ridge five hundred yards above us.

Without taking his eyes off the now-smoldering tree, Paul said, almost to himself, "What happened there is a lot like life."

I nodded and waited for the explanation that always followed statements like that from Paul.

"That old tree has struggled to take root and grow and stand tall. To anchor itself against wind and weather. To reach to the heavens, so it might shelter the seedlings that sprout around it," he said.

There followed a long silence, broken only by the falling rain and the soft moan of the wind through the forest. Then Paul continued. "I hope when the lightning bolts of life come your way, you'll be like that old tree, still standing when the smoke clears."

I didn't say anything, but Paul sensed my puzzlement and went on to say, "I do a few things I shouldn't in the eyes of the Maker. But I think He'll look at both sides of the coin and make a fair judgment. I'm sure glad I have to face Him on Judgment Day and not some of my neighbors."

Again the silence came, broken only by the rain and the occasional clap of thunder and flash of lightning. A thin wisp of smoke still curled up and was carried off by the winds that buffeted the old tree and the ridgetop.

Paul continued, "I think the Lord is like that old tree and the lightning, thunder, and rain when it comes to dealing with us. He warns us, like the thunder speaking, and then on occasion He knocks us upside the head with a fire bolt, but He always sends the rain to create new hope and new beginnings and to put out the fire.

"The trick is to have our roots dug in and to grab hold of the things that will help us come out of life's lightning strikes still standing. Don't matter much what the neighbors say and perceive if you can say I'm trying to do the best I can; then walk your talk."

That day comes back to me when I hear certain people judging others. Paul's wise words have served as a brake of sorts on my own tongue and have helped me learn patience. They've also motivated me to cultivate my own roots in the core values that sustain people on the windswept ridges of life. It reminds me, too, that the cooling rains of hope, of new beginnings, of forgiveness and love will stamp out the fires of adversity as we turn to Him. He always sends the rain.

Small-Town Fund Raiser

Where there's a need, there's a way—sometimes.

All the ingredients were there: a World War II surplus radar gun, a set of walkie-talkies, and the upcoming opening day of fishing season. Add to that a willing justice of the peace and an obscure speed-limit sign placed well outside the edge of the town where the highway to Utah's best fishery passed through, and you had the basics for a fund raiser—a speed trap for "them city slickers."

A couple of other technicalities had to be overcome to get into the wallets of "them outsiders." The town, like most rural communities of a-couple-hundred-or-so residents, had no need for a full-time marshal. That could be taken care of by the mayor and a town-council resolution establishing marshal and justice-of-the-peace offices with a few "deputies."

With all that in place, the plan was simple: catch those speeding fishermen on the radar gun, stop them, issue a ticket, and then send them to the justice, who just happened to be in for the occasion.

What made this a natural fund raiser was the fact that, back then, Utah had an opening day for fishing. Unlike today's yearlong season, no fishing was permitted for several months of the year, and thousands flocked to the waters when the season began. Most made it a family camp-out and headed for the lakes and streams for a long weekend.

So it was with some wonder that, on my way to the lake, I found myself at the end of a long line of vehicles stretching back from the town's edge. I could see two or three men walking back, talking to each of the drivers of the stopped cars and trucks. Clad in blue-denim bib overalls, the men appeared to hand a paper of some sort to some of the drivers before waving them on. Before and after each conversation, the men appeared to be talking to someone.

Everything came into sharp focus as Owen, a man I recognized, approached my truck talking into one of those walkie-talkies. Clad in his usual farm-chore clothing, he had a silver star-shaped badge pinned to his bib.

"Know how fast you were going?" Owen questioned.

"Why?" I responded, still wondering why all this was unfolding, delaying everyone's journey to the campsite near the water.

"Got ya at fifty-five in a thirty-five," Owen stated in his most authoritative tone of voice.

"Ya got me with what?" I countered.

"We got ya on the radar gun. Just take this ticket to the judge at the Merc, and he'll handle things so ya can go on," Owen instructed. That's when I remembered the old farm truck parked back there with its driver pointing a contraption of some sort at passing traffic.

Looking at the "ticket," I saw a description of my truck, its license plate number, and the numbers 55/35. "Wait a minute," I said. "Show me the evidence. I have a right to see the evidence." By that time it was clear to me that the "evidence" had been erased two or three times on those behind me.

"You got anyone who knows if your radar gun is right?" I questioned.

"Tell it to the judge," Owen snorted. Then he hesitated and snatched the "ticket" from my hand. "Yer a smart one, ain't ya?" he declared. Then, stuffing the slip of paper into his pocket, he ordered, "Go on. I'll give ya a break this time, but slow down."

I was too late to save my brother Lane. He, like so many others, ponied up and made a contribution to the fund raiser. Needless to say, the event made the local newspaper, and the spotlight of indignation burned bright.

Like me, others questioned the fund-raiser equipment, the qualifications of the deputies, and the motives for the event. Nearly everyone took an alternate route in the days to come as the operation went public. The radar gun and the walkie-talkies went on the shelf, and the posse was disbanded.

Today, all of that has been replaced by old police vehicles, mannequins dressed in police uniforms sitting behind their steering wheels, positioned at the entrance to rural communities. Still, the fund raisers haven't completely disappeared. Every now and then, a part-time town marshal can be found lurking in the shadows, keeping the town's budget balanced. This usually occurs on weekends when those who've been to the country are headed home to the big city.

The fact that the city limits to many of Utah's small rural communities may stretch out over a mile or more, with homes here and there along the way, puts big-city drivers and their wallets in jeopardy. And the fact that law enforcement for these small towns is part-time also causes locals to forget—all a great recipe for two or three fund raisers on high-traffic holiday weekends.

Like the justice of the peace told one complaining fisherman: "When there's a need, there's a way."

Sern

There are two kinds of personal power:
one comes by virtue of what *you are,*
the other by virtue of who *you are.*

When I was a young man in my teens, probably fifteen or sixteen hundred people lived in my hometown of Ephraim, Utah. Looking back, it occurs to me that we probably had our fair share of single adult-male residents.

Some had failed marriages, and many found themselves alone or living with their aging mothers. They were farmers, sheepherders, businessmen, and day workers. Among them were college-degree holders and semi-illiterates.

While some fought the demons of alcohol, others shunned living too close to their neighbors. It was a curious mix of humanity.

There was Milt, Sern, Tut-Tut, Rattler, Jimmy, Isaac, Whit, Sad and Sorry (brothers), the Bear Cub brothers, Benny, Roy, He Eagle, Deaf Johnny, the Buck brothers, and Frank. I'm certain that time has erased others from the pages of my memory, but these men were as much a part of the town mosaic as Main Street itself.

It is said that good things are where you find them. In the lives of this group of men resides a compelling argument that the core of our existence is not in what we have but in what we are. Sometimes what we are, like the earth's treasures of gold and silver, is often disguised; it can be there, just under our noses, but we don't see it.

I don't think the community at large saw these men from a positive viewpoint, but life has a way of teaching us that things aren't always what they appear to be. And sometimes we only learn that when life jumps up and slaps us on the side of the head. Sometimes we learn it as a result of a lifetime of little experiences that suddenly turn on the light of understanding. And sometimes we never get the message.

Part of the problem is that we like to generalize, to lump things together, and put people in neat little boxes. You belong to the church, or you don't belong. You're active, or you're inactive. You're part of the social network, or you fit in somewhere else.

To that end, like all of God's creatures, among these men were the weak and the strong. The strong were given their own space and went their own way with little visible opposition or care. They neither asked for nor received much in the way of community fellowship or involvement.

The weak, too, did not expose themselves to the community at large. They carefully chose the risks involved in venturing beyond their own boundaries.

And when it came time to leave their worldly cares behind, there was, for most of these men, little notice. Their passing, except within their immediate families, caused little more notice than the shift in the breeze that came out of the canyon at dusk. No one asked about the property they left behind, and their obituaries offered little more than essential statistics: name, born/died, member of the Church of Jesus Christ, son of, burial will be, and so on. Like most of "the other Mormons," the inactive, they went back to the church for burial services and the fulfillment of His admonition that "Inasmuch as ye have done it unto one of the least of these my brethren, ye have done it unto me" (Matt. 25:40).

When Sern died, I decided that I needed to go to his viewing and funeral. There wouldn't be a big crowd there, but that wasn't the reason I felt compelled to go. I went because Sern, like a lot of the other loners I've mentioned, had invested in me.

Sern was a slender, bespectacled man who always had a book in hand. He walked everywhere he went, accompanied by his black-and-white collie-looking dog. College educated and a loner in the adult community, Sern spent hour upon hour at the city library. He was a mathematical genius and knew a great deal about many more things besides. If knowledge can be counted as wealth, Sern left this world a rich man.

Curious about his choice to live life as he did, I asked Sern why, given his wealth of knowledge, he didn't pursue money and material riches; surely he could have done that. His response was a simple truth that few men grasp in its entirety. Without looking up, Sern told me, "Life is not just about making money and acquiring property. There is no lasting legacy in that. It's the good we do for others that transcends our time here."

Sern wasn't on the Snow College payroll, but he probably taught algebra, geometry, physics, and calculus to as many students as the professors did. Class was in session most weeknights at the public library. Like many others, I went to him to get his one-on-one tutoring when the day's lessons at school had gone over my head. Sern prepared a lot of students for exam days and took quiet satisfaction in hearing their test results. Going back over any missed problems was mandatory. That was, according to Sern, "necessary if you wanted more than just a grade from a class."

I guess I shouldn't have been surprised when on the day of Sern's funeral the chapel seats began to fill up. If I'd really thought about it, I would have known that his legacy was being fulfilled that day—that, in his own words, "It's the good we do for others that transcends our time here."

Tooley Hoot

Little eyes watch us all the time,
and little ears listen to us more than we think.

THE MAN I knew only as Tooley Hoot lived on a farm that his dad, his dad's dad, and his great-grandpa had raised a family on. It wasn't the best soil for raising crops, and sometimes water was lacking. Nevertheless, like so many who scratched a living from the land, Tooley Hoot followed in the family tradition, first together with his dad and then alone, when his mom and dad were gone.

He was the son who stayed on the land, caring for it and his aging parents, while his brothers and sisters migrated to greener pastures. Not until a series of unexpected events unfolded did things change dramatically for Tooley Hoot.

The first of these occurred when a man caught up with Tooley Hoot as he was pushing his cows to spring pasture. "I'm looking to buy a place like this," the stranger informed Tooley Hoot.

"Ain't for sale," came the blunt reply.

"Well, won't you at least let me visit with you when you're not busy... hear me out?" the stranger asked.

"Ain't no use, but if'n it'll make ya feel better, stop by about dark."

Well, while pushing those cows and calves, Tooley Hoot got to thinking. *Wonder what this place is worth? I ain't gitten' any younger, and I don't have anyone to pass it on to. Might as well listen.*

One thing led to another, and the sale was agreed to with one condition: Tooley Hoot would keep the house and a few acres for a horse or two and a place to keep a century's worth of antique farm and ranch equipment.

Tooley Hoot put the money in the bank—more money than three generations before him had earned or dreamed about earning on the old homestead.

With time now on his hands and feeling kind of lonely, Tooley Hoot went to town a couple of nights a week to rub shoulders at the senior citizen center. There he met a widow, and they hit it off. Next thing Tooley Hoot knew, he was married and had a family: wife, adult stepchildren, and grandkids. Life was good.

Then one day it got better. Like the man who bought the ranch, another with a pocketful of money wanted to buy Tooley Hoot's antique farm equipment. A deal was struck, and Tooley Hoot put the money in the bank.

Shortly after, however, Tooley Hoot got a reality check. He was out fishing with one of the grandkids when the boy asked, "Grandpa, can you croak like a frog?"

Somewhat surprised by the question, Tooley Hoot responded, "No, I can't. Why do you ask?"

To that, the boy replied, "Well, Mom says that if you croaked, we'd all be filthy rich."

I've always wondered how that revelation might have played into Tooley Hoot's will. Something to think about. Always, it seems, there are unintended consequences.

No Window

Live the good life: laugh and imagine.

THE WORKING LANGUAGE of my hometown in the '50s always left something to the imagination. When it came down to describing the behavior, character, or intellectual capacity of his counterparts, a native son of Sanpete County offered listeners a word picture and left the rest to his audience.

This always gave the listener food for thought and was good for stimulating intellectual growth and problem-solving skills. For instance, when the "subject" of conversation was said to be "a brick shy of a full load," you had to visualize someone not quite complete, someone who might be lacking a bit on the intellectual side. But, as everyone knows, "close" only counts in horseshoes.

If the "topic of discussion" was "a half bubble off center," it could mean that the subject just needed a little adjustment in his or her thinking. Nothing serious that a trip to the woodshed wouldn't fix.

On the other hand, if one were "a quart low on the dipstick," there was cause for concern. Being a quart low, you had to assume one of two things: first, that the person in question had never been at full operating capacity, so you shouldn't expect much, or second, that the intellectual process was too taxing, and the wear and tear was consuming brain cells. In either case, you would make allowances and remember what once was.

If people tended to do things on impulse or their behavior was off the wall, they might not be "playing with a full deck." Thus, you should never expect the laws of chance to apply and could come to accept strange behavior on a consistent basis.

If the speaker really had the conviction that the condition of the subject was extreme and irreversible, the description of that poor soul would run toward things like "The light's on, but nobody's home," "The needle is on empty," or "There's nothing between the ears to stop the wind."

Nicknames were important in my hometown. If you didn't have one, you just weren't part of the community. Anyone asking for someone by his given name had to be a stranger. And more often than not, a local wouldn't know who the stranger had referred to. There were, for example, three clans of Olsens: the Haigs, the Keskos, and Ole's Sons. Individual nicknames were everywhere, and to be referred to by your own name usually meant you were being addressed by your mother, grandmother, or the bishop.

Nicknames, some of which I've mentioned earlier and recall with a sense of reverence, include the following: "Liberty Bell," who was "half-cracked"; the "Red Baron," who buzzed around town in a Piper Cub; the "Cattle Baron," who owned a "vast" herd of thirty to forty Herefords; "Sad" and "Sorry," who were brothers—one *sad* because he wasn't married, and the other *sorry* because he *was*; "Iron Tail," named in deference to a certain anatomical endowment (which left no one in doubt as to how he got his name); "Scissors," the local barber; "Black Bart," who owned and operated a welding and machine shop; "Obtuse," the geometry teacher; "Cannonball," the woodshop and Future Farmers of America teacher who was built like one; and the "Bear Cubs," brothers who seldom shaved or bathed. A sheepherder who flew high when he came to town was "He Eagle," and there was even a night rider named "Coyote" who sat in the shadows on his swaybacked pony.

There were others, but looking back, I guess I'd have to say that an important part of my education came from the mental exercise and problem-solving skills that deciphering such word pictures required.

One of our more colorful native sons worked in a local meat shop. Milt Beal was a word-picture artist in the highest sense of the word. One day he sold a couple of stewing hens to a female acquaintance and assured her they'd been fresh killed that day. A short time later, she burst through the shop door, chickens in hand, screaming, "Milt, you said these chickens were fresh!" Before Milt could respond, she dropped one hen on the cutting block, and thrust the second chicken's rear end over Milt's nose and mouth. Jerking his nose from the cavity where the chicken's innards had been removed, Milt shot back, "But, but, but, ma'am, even Marilyn Monroe couldn't pass that test!"

On another occasion, Milt was asked how his only son was doing. Milt informed the inquirer, "The boy not only doesn't have a pot to pee in but also doesn't have a window to throw it out of, either!"

As I mentioned earlier, the working language of the people in my hometown always left something to the imagination of the listener. Times were hard in the Sanpitch Valley then, and I think that's the reason why vocabulary was as it was. People used their own brand of humor to bring smiles and amusement into their lives. The ability to elicit laughter in others gives one power, and the person with this power can perform miracles. He can heal wounded souls and mend broken spirits.

Today, we've become a people without much homespun humor. We've lost something by being so self-conscious, so politically correct. Humor today is a very deliberate act. I'm glad I grew up when I did and where I did. Spontaneous language and humor that existed in the shadows of the Sanpitch Valley represented an art form. That kind of art comes from a deeper source somewhere; it's part of the act of just living, as in "Let's make the best of things and enjoy the ride while we pass this way. Who knows, we may never travel this way again, so let's take the good memories—and the laughter—with us."

The Party Line

In small towns, news travels at the speed of the party line.

In the good ol' days, about 1940 to 1945 BCC (before computers and cell phones), those who had phones (not everyone did) had a boxlike unit that hung on the wall. It had a cone-shaped receptacle to talk into and a couple of small bells above it to signal incoming calls. On the side of the box was an earpiece that hung on a hook. If you cut off the top half of a Coke bottle, you'd have something resembling the shape of the phone's handheld unit.

When we got our phone in the late 1950s, there were six other parties on our line. We were at the end of the line, so we had to be educated with respect to identifying the number of rings that would signal a call for us. Sometimes more than one person on the line misheard the ring count and structure and answered the phone by mistake.

Some of those sharing a line made it a practice to quietly listen in, snooping and eavesdropping on the traffic of the party line. We had one of those: Alice. She was at the head of the line. Her ring was one long ring and then one short ring, which would repeat several times until she answered.

When Alice eavesdropped on others' calls, she would sometimes get so engrossed in the conversation that she'd actually join in. Most of the time Alice just listened quietly, but even that could be difficult for her.

On one occasion, my older sister and her girlfriend were talking on the phone. When my sister realized she could hear heavy breathing on the line, she said, "You can hang up now, Alice!"

"I'm not listening!" came the spontaneous reply from Alice in her most indignant tone of voice.

Another time, one of the women on the line who was in charge of an upcoming church dinner was discussing the menu with a caller who was also on the dinner committee. As they discussed whom they should invite to bring certain foods to the occasion, Alice interjected herself into the conversation, saying, "Don't bother calling me unless I can bring my extra-special potato salad."

Alice was, in her opinion, qualified to offer advice on a wide range of topics and situations. As was sometimes the case, she would pick up the phone to listen in on a conversation that had been going on for some time before she joined in. On one occasion, two women were discussing their work, and one mentioned that she had a typewriter that needed some maintenance. Alice quietly and slowly picked up the phone and heard the woman with the typewriter problems say, "My *P*, colon, and period don't work. I need to have someone repair them."

That's when Alice interjected with the following advice: "Don't be going to any quack doctor. All you need to do is drink a cup of Brigham tea a couple times a day, and all that woman stuff will clear right up!"

In retrospect, with all the uproar about government snooping, we didn't have to invest millions in cybersnooping technology. All we needed were a few Alices and the simplicity of the party line. There were few secrets—but a good supply of gossip—in the good ol' days.

If Anything Can Go Wrong, It Will (Murphy's Law)

If it happens, it must be possible.

TRAPPING HAS ALWAYS been a part of the American story. The trappers were the ones who pushed the frontier boundaries west. The fur from the trappers' harvest was important to the economy then, and it still flourishes in a worldwide market.

My family connection to trapping goes back four generations, each passing on the skills of the trade to the next. One of those skills is scent making. Just as the fragrances of today's perfumes are designed to captivate the senses, the *trapper's perfume* creates interest and inspires the animal to investigate the source. This story has its beginnings here.

My brother received a call from a fellow trapper requesting a jar of his special, secret-formula *trapper's perfume.* Arrangements were made for the delivery. My brother would drop off a jar of the good stuff at a mutual friend's place of business first thing the following morning. All went according to plan except for one small detail: the business was closed. A quick phone call remedied that: the *perfume* (scent) would be left at the back door, out of the way, to be picked up a bit later.

So it was that the jar with the salsa label filled with *trapper's perfume* was left at the designated pickup spot. Among its other ingredients, the scent recipe called for a touch of skunk essence. At this point, the law of unintended consequences takes over—that is, if anything can go wrong, it will!

Well, here's how it all went down. Shortly after the *perfume* was left there in the salsa jar, the business opened and a van pulled into the back parking lot. Its driver was a guard from the nearby prison who went inside to speak to the business owner. That left the van's other occupants—a group of trustee inmates—waiting in the van. One of the inmates spotted the salsa jar.

As they say, "curiosity killed the cat." The more the inmate stared at the salsa jar, the more tempting the thought of jumping out and retrieving it became. The guard was a "good guy," and with a bottle of salsa in hand, he would surely stop and pick up a bag of chips they could enjoy with it on the way home.

Well, the plan worked. With chips and salsa to share, the ride back to the prison would be a treat. Remember, now—if anything can go wrong, it will. Turns out my brother had really cinched tight the lid to the "salsa" jar—and then some—in order to keep the contents and aroma inside. Essence of spotted skunk can be detected on the wind miles away from the source.

So it was that the jar was passed around in futile attempts to open it. That was, until the biggest inmate, who was seated in the front passenger seat, said, "Here, let me show you how a real man handles stuff." With that, he held the jar horizontally and twisted the lid with all his might. When the lid came off, a good portion of the "salsa" came out, landing in his lap. Essence of skunk immediately filled the van, and the jar was tossed into the driver's lap, then into the backseat, and then back up front. With each exchange, more "salsa" came out of the jar, bringing with it a horrific stream of cursing, gagging, and upchucking.

The "salsa" bottle didn't stop rolling until the van ended up in the brush alongside of the road. As the driver managed to stop the van, the doors flew open, and the occupants scrambled to exit and escape the vile demon that had been thrust among them. Passersby watched in awe, wondering what was happening, as the men stood about in various degrees of undress, having rid themselves of their "salsa"-stained clothing while standing right there next to the highway.

When last seen, the van and its occupants had made their way to a car wash for an unintended bath. I heard that the inmates were placed in solitary confinement until the "perfume" dissipated, and the driver was placed on an unscheduled leave of absence.

If anything can go wrong, it will!

Frank and Dog

Loyalty is a two-way street
where good deeds never come back alone.

Frank was a bachelor who lived by himself on the old O. C. Doak farm between Manti and Ephraim. He and his dog had come to town on the 4:00 p.m. freight train, like so many who were searching for a better life hard on the heels of the Great Depression.

We lived a mile south of Ephraim, and Frank was our neighbor, another two miles to the south. As mentioned earlier, my brothers and I used to walk the highway picking up Coke and beer bottles, which we sold for a penny each to get a show ticket or a box of .22 bullets. Sometimes the money went toward the price of a sack of flour. It was on one of these bottle-gathering expeditions that I first met Frank. The relationship would last until I was twenty-one, some ten years hence.

Frank liked his coffee and always offered a cup to anyone who might happen by. He also liked his "roll-yer-own" Bull Durham smokes. His salt-and-pepper beard was stained a brownish yellow where the tobacco smoke curled away from the corners of his mouth.

He had no car or truck and, as far as I knew, no family ties. If Frank had a last name, I never heard it while he was alive.

Frank earned his room and board by doing chores and keeping an eye on the farm and animals. Everywhere he went, an old black-and-white sheepdog was by his side.

I had the opportunity to work an occasional Saturday for O. C. Doak during the winter and spring and then ten days or so during the summer. After two or three years of that routine, Frank began to reveal bits and pieces about his identity. He'd come to town, he said, because he preferred a solitary life over the dog-eat-dog world he'd escaped from.

I don't know what Frank's station in life had been in that dog-eat-dog world, but I do know that he knew a lot of things about life and human behavior. He was always giving us valuable lessons based on what was taking place around us. One thing I learned was that dogs speak in body language. Dog—that's what he called the black-and-white sheepdog—was aggressive in my presence at first. Frank told me he was just being "a little protective."

Later, when I would enter the yard, Dog would wag his tail ever so lightly and stretch out in a long, low bow and then stand up and do it several more times as he inched toward me. Seeing this, Frank said, "Dog says, 'Hello, it's good to see you.'"

"With dogs, what you see is what you get," Frank explained. "They don't play the games we people get into."

As I said earlier, Frank revealed himself grudgingly and, in the eyes of this boy, was a mystery, a puzzle with missing pieces. He had risked before and had not found his trust well placed. Now, he figured the safe thing to do was to retreat within himself—a tough road for sure. Nonetheless, the hurt of the past insulated him from any desire to return to paths once traveled.

Frank wasn't part of the mainstream of humanity, but he was very humane. You could tell by the way he treated the animals in his charge that, through his eyes, they were God's creatures and deserved the same care a loving father would give one of his own.

As the years went by, I tried to stay in touch with Frank, and when I was drafted into the army in the midst of the Korean War, I made it a point to visit Frank and say, "So long." It was the last time I would see him.

When I returned home two years later, he was gone. His time had come, and he'd gone to meet his Maker. When I asked about Frank in town, as near as I could tell, nobody seemed to know much or care much.

When I stopped at the timeworn redbrick farmhouse a few days after I got home, the old black sheepdog came to the gate to meet me.

"Dog," I called, "it's been a long time."

He came up close, sniffed at my hand, and went into his old stretch-and-bow routine.

"Hello to you too, Dog," I whispered. "I've been a far piece since I saw you last."

The doors to the old house with the curling, faded wood shingles were open. The stench of sheep drifted on the cold January air as Dog and I went inside. A dozen of the woolly creatures jumped up and scrambled for the back door at our intrusion.

In the kitchen, the old coffeepot with its broken handle and blackened sides still sat on the back of the old Monarch woodburning stove.

Frank had lived in the kitchen during the cold winter months, when the old stove was the only source of heat. Dog went over to the old bed in the corner and climbed up on the mattress where he and Frank had kept each other company on many cold, lonely, winter nights. His eyes followed me as I opened a drawer or two in the cupboard.

On the backside of the door where the sheep had exited hung a pair of Frank's old blue-denim bib overalls, a tattered wool coat, and an old black cap with tie-up ear flaps. A small nail served as their anchor.

The old coffeepot, the coat, the hat, the faded blue-denim bibs, and Dog appeared to be the only signs that Frank had existed.

Half to myself, half to Dog, I thought out loud, "Hell of a way to go!" With that, I turned to leave and called to Dog. "Come on, Dog. You can come and live with me."

Dog lifted his head, but he didn't move.

Again, I called to him and patted the side of my leg in encouragement. This time Dog got up and followed me to the gate. I opened the door of the pickup and again called to Dog.

"Come on, boy, let's go home."

Dog had dropped his backside in the snow and just sat there at the gate. Then he turned his head back to the house, looked at me, got up, and trotted back to where we'd come from. It was then, as I watched Dog disappear around the corner of the house, that I understood Dog's refusal to leave the home he had shared with Frank. While others could feed Dog and the sheep and pick up Frank's chores, no one could fill the void his passing had created for Dog.

It was then, too, that what I'd heard Frank say after almost every victory and every defeat in the face of life's challenges became clear to me.

I could hear his words and silently repeated them to myself as Dog disappeared into the house he'd shared with Frank: "Anything worth anything costs something."

I'd heard Frank say those words after staying up all night with a sick lamb. I'd heard those words after we'd stayed with the first water turn for three days, almost nonstop, to get the water through the newly planted fields. I'd heard them when I said good-bye before leaving for the Korean War—wondering why.

Dog heard them, too! His loyalty to the man who'd given him companionship, trust, and security remained intact, even in the face of life alone.

"Anything worth anything costs something!"

Addendum

After writing Frank's story, I began to search for his grave. Long story short, he lies in an unmarked grave in the Manti City Cemetery. Because his was a pauper's burial provided by the county, the grave has no headstone or marker, and that makes placing one in the right place problematic.

An Internet search revealed that Frank had immigrated to America from Austria. The trail ended there. Perhaps it's just as well. As I mentioned above, Frank never shared a last name or spoke of his past or family. He was very guarded in that respect, so it seems right to honor his wish to leave the past in the past—an unspoken confidence honored.

Willie

The obvious and the hidden often walk hand in hand.

A LOT OF things were taken for granted in my hometown. Everyone pretty much knew everyone else, as well as their habits and routines as they went about their daily business.

Some, I've heard, believed the difference between a rut and a groove was about a quarter of an inch. Willie, a homegrown farmer, considered himself in a groove. The rhythms of his comings and goings were fine-tuned, he thought, to the heartbeat of the entire community.

Willie, therefore, was just a little more than upset when the town marshal, "Despert Hespert," sometimes known as the "Iron Claw," issued Willie a citation for making a left-hand turn in front of oncoming traffic—the oncoming traffic being Despert Hespert.

"Not guilty!" Willie emphatically pleaded on his day in court. The justice of the peace asked why Willie believed he was innocent.

"Hell, Yer Honor." Willie snorted. "Any damn fool knows I always turn there!" Willie got off with a suspended five-dollar fine.

On another occasion, Willie hired a helper, a young man named Rollin. They got along just great until one night Willie came to town in his old pickup with the remains of a wire gate draped around the front end. Willie pulled into Dewey's service station, where he was asked about the tangle of wire and wood.

"Dammit," Willie fumed, "I told that knothead to open the gate!"

Willie could be a mite forgetful on occasion. One night at about ten o'clock, Rollin's mother knocked on Willie's door. When Willie answered, Mom inquired as to Rollin's whereabouts, as he hadn't come home.

"Dammit!" Willie exclaimed. "I knew I'd fergot somethin'! But don't worry, he can't get lost. We were cleaning the well, and I fergot to bring him up. He'll be right where I left him."

That fall, Willie and Rollin went up the mountain to get a load of poles for a new corral. They took the big team of look-alike workhorses up there to skid the poles to the loading point.

Along about midday, Willie felled a big aspen tree on top of one of the horses, breaking the horse's leg. The horse went down and refused to get up. Willie then ordered Rollin to tie the horses to a tree and go with him to town to get a gun.

"We'll have to shoot the son of a bitch," he informed the boy.

Off they went. Returning several hours later, Willie dispatched the horse lying on the ground. At the roar of the rifle, the other horse, standing nearby, bolted. But not far. Its broken leg wouldn't let it.

Willie looked at the dead horse and then at the crippled horse, exclaiming, "You dumb son of a bitch! Just for that I'm going to have to shoot you, too." He did.

Some who'd known Willie most of his life said that he, like so many who served their country with distinction in World War II, came home a changed man. He wasn't alone. A town of perhaps fifteen hundred citizens, Ephraim had at least twenty men who'd returned from the battlefront, had never married or had troubled marriages, and essentially became loners in the community. For many, alcohol was their escape. Others, like Willie, had their capricious and erratic moments. That being said, the men I knew personally, Willie included, always stood at attention, saluted the flag at the Fourth of July parade, and held back a tear as old memories came flooding to the surface.

The lesson here is that, in the journey of life, the hidden and the obvious often sit side by side, and it takes more than the judgment of our eyes to find the truth.

The He Eagle (a.k.a. Lee Tiny)

Recognizing our mistakes is the first step forward.

Like some Difference Makers in my life, at first glance Lee would seem to be an unlikely candidate to effect change in a positive way—an easy conclusion to come to because he appeared to be everything society and mainstream culture frowned upon. He had a drinking problem, was overweight, was sometimes loud, and seemed to always be in the way.

Sometime later I would discover that those impressions were indicative of his "winter" identity. They were seasonal and came and went like spring and summer follow winter. Lee was a sheepherder, and it was in that role that his direction and purpose in life led him to abandon his winter ways.

Like just about everyone else, Lee had a nickname. In fact, he had two of them: Lee Tiny and the He Eagle. The first was a not-so-subtle reference to his excess weight. The second referred to the fact that come summer, he seemed to be able to detach himself from the rest of the world as some male eagles do.

He had other things in common with the great bird. I've watched eagles feed on roadkill rabbit and deer, seemingly oblivious to the crows and magpies underfoot squawking insults at them. More than once I've followed an eagle's journey across blue skies, two or more small birds dogging its flight and nipping at its tail feathers. In response, the big bird just held a steady course of flight until its tormentors tired of the game.

The He Eagle, like his namesake, seemed not to notice when the "birds" of the human species dogged his flight through life.

In the beginning, life had been promising for Lee. In his youth he'd been athletic, muscular, and quick. Baseball, basketball, and football came easy for him. I'm told there was a time when he held many of the records that define excellence in those sports as he went through high school and Snow College.

Basketball, however, was his passion. Long after his playing days were over, Lee could be found in the front row at midcourt, cheering for the home team. He was there as I played for Snow High School and Snow College. During warm-ups and at half time, we high-fived and got some coaching from him but kept our distance from the smell of wine on his breath. During the game, the He Eagle could be heard above the crowd noise as he implored the team again and again with "Come on, Snow!" In retrospect, that behavior was fueled by his love for the game but triggered by the alcohol.

Summers found the He Eagle high upon the ridges and meadows of Skyline Drive with his band of sheep. It was there that he left the winter side of his life behind. It was there, too, that I would discover a man as different as night and day from the one I'd laughed with, teased a little, and wondered about due to some of his behavior midcourt.

Lee's horse had fallen with Lee in the saddle. The result of that mishap was a broken arm, and the sheep's owner thought he needed some help up there. I was that help.

When the boss and I arrived at camp, Lee protested that he could "damn well handle things." Nonetheless, wanted or not, I would spend most of a month with him. It was like boot camp—early to bed, early to rise; a place for everything, and everything in its place. The animals came first, and we fit in somewhere down the line. Take care of the little details, and the big ones will fall into place.

Still, little was said about basketball or any of the other team sports I tried to strike up a conversation about. That puzzled me. He knew I was a basketball player, as I'd spoken with him on occasion when he would show up to watch practice. But that all changed a day or two before I was to leave Lee on his own again.

We were doing the supper dishes, and I thanked Lee for letting me work with him. I told him I looked forward to seeing him at half-court when winter arrived. For a long time, I received no response other than a slight nod of his head.

We finished the dishes in silence, and Lee climbed out of the sheep wagon. He did a last-minute before-dark check of the horses, dogs, and sheep, as he always did before going to bed.

When he came back in, he said, almost in a whisper, "Keeze, I'm going to miss your company." That took me aback, and I wondered if I'd heard him correctly. It was my turn to nod in acknowledgment.

"You remind me of myself when I was your age. Life was in front of me then, and I only had to make the right choices," he continued.

Again, I responded with silence but gave a more emphatic nod of agreement. Then, without looking at me, he again whispered almost to himself, "Some choices pay us back, while other choices make us pay."

He went on, "In the beginning, I chose to drink. Now the booze chooses me. It happens every fall when I bring the herd off the mountain. That first choice could have made all the difference, but I didn't know that I'd have to pay for that choice then—not until it was too late. I've been paying ever since."

Then, looking straight into my eyes, he concluded, "Keeze, I guess the point of all this is that we all have choices. Some big, some small—but they all matter and need to be made on the basis of pay or get paid."

That philosophy—pay or get paid—is very powerful in its simplicity, and over the years the wisdom of the He Eagle in that moment of reflection has stood the test of time in my own life. That summer experience, with all of its structure, order, and rewards, stood in sharp contrast to the winter version of the He Eagle. It was an early lesson in judgment and a testament to the fact that the obvious and the hidden often reside side by side on the path of life.

Looking back, I'm grateful that I got to see the hidden, the summer side of this man, who in his own words had left a boy with the truth of the Savior's admonition that "whatsoever a man soweth, that shall he also reap" (Gal. 6:7).

Fritz

Anything worth anything costs something.

FRITZ, ACCORDING TO *Webster's Dictionary*, is a term whose origin is unknown. The word's meaning is defined as "a state of disorder or disrepair."

We needed a dog for the upcoming pheasant hunt, so my brother Lane, a member of the Orem Fire Department, asked Ralph, the local dogcatcher, to be on the lookout for a likely candidate. Days went by with no prospects in sight.

Then the night before opening day, Ralph delivered Fritz. The old dog, a German shorthaired pointer, was definitely down on his luck. Like the old saying, Fritz hadn't had a square meal since Old Ring, an ageless dog, was pup.

Ralph was apologetic. "Sorry I couldn't come up with something better. If his nose and pointer are on the fritz, just put him out of his misery."

The words were no sooner uttered than the dog cocked his leg and sprinkled on Ralph's boot and pant leg. Needless to say, that part of the old hound was *not* on the fritz.

That act, however, won the instant admiration and applause of the fire-station crew. And, naturally, they dubbed him "Fritz."

Ralph left, muttering something like, "The SOB was supposed to be man's best friend." Fritz got a hero's welcome, and when the crew shared supper with him, he showed his appreciation by letting off the rankest farts ever experienced at Station One. Attempts to remove him from beneath the kitchen table were met with a low growl.

We loaded old Fritz into the trunk of my '55 Chevy and headed down the highway toward the old hometown and surrounding fields. We hadn't been on the road long when the foulest odor known to man or beast filled the cab.

After first accusing each other, we finally determined that old Fritz was trying to tell us something. The windows came down, but only briefly. It was too cold. Besides, the draft from the open windows seemed to suck more of the foul air from the trunk.

We decided that we'd bring the dog up front in the hope that a partially open window would spare us the burning nostrils and itching eyes. As soon as Fritz was snuggled on the floor in front of the heater, the farts stopped and the window could go up. Fritz always rode in the front seat after that.

Once we took to the field, we soon discovered what we'd begun to suspect: this was no ordinary dog. Fritz took over the hunt. He investigated every bit of cover, every place a pheasant might hide. His point was textbook perfect. Always, the dog stayed at just the right distance and hunted for everyone behind him. He retrieved downed birds with hardly a ruffled feather. A wave of the hand, a word, and he complied in robot-like fashion.

By midmorning, Fritz could tinkle wherever he wanted and fart anytime he wanted. Somehow that side of the dog's personality could be tolerated in exchange for the servant-like, almost benevolent transformation in the field and on the hunt.

It was like ol' Fritz was saying, "OK, I'll hunt and do the dirty work, but you guys know who's in charge. If you want to dance, you got to pay the fiddler!"

By noon, Fritz had done his part, and we had our limit of birds. As soon as the last bird was delivered, Fritz headed for the ranch. I think he could count and knew we were done.

The next day, we went back to the fields. We were working some sagebrush and salt grass when the local warden, Tut-Tut, appeared on the scene. Due to his sneaky ways, Tut-Tut wasn't the best-liked game warden. He wasn't known as much of a hunter either. Word had it among the locals that the only thing he'd ever killed was a six-pack. In fact, someone marked the spot of that feat by inscribing words to that effect on an aspen tree in Six Mile Canyon.

Now, Tut-Tut knew that every one of us had a license to hunt. He'd checked that out several times on the just-completed elk-and-deer hunts. Still, he stopped our current hunt to "check yer licenses, boys."

Ol' Fritz had been letting us know that birds were in front of us. When birds were close, his tail went crazy. At the precise moment Warden Tut-Tut stopped the hunt; Fritz went on point. Ordinarily he would have held that point until the cows came home. This time, however, after locking on the bird for several minutes, he pounced on the rooster and delivered it to us. About that time, Warden Tut-Tut made a big mistake. He commented, "That scroungy old mutt got a hunting license? I could arrest and jail him, ya know."

Knowing some of the tales about Tut-Tut's attempts to make an arrest, we dummied up. But not ol' Fritz! He just circled in behind the warden and lifted his leg.

Funny thing happened after that. As long as that old dog was with us, Tut-Tut never bothered to check our licenses again.

Silence Speaks

Listen to silence, the source of great wisdom and strength.

My dad was, among other things, a sheepherder. When he was with sheep, he often took one of my brothers or me onto the mountain, where we lived in a tent or the luxury of a sheep wagon. While there, we learned the ways of the mountain and the wild creatures that lived there. We also learned that silence speaks.

It speaks of respect. When the fires of life bring heartache, anguish, and mourning into our lives, a caring touch and a hug—just being there—are more powerful than words.

Silence can also be a great peacemaker. Unkind words left unspoken will over time die a tranquil death. How we express our feelings is just as important as the fact that we expressed them at all. Deeds speaking of love require few words.

The need for silence in our lives is as vital as breathing. Without it, our spirit withers and dies. We must have it to nourish strength and wisdom. Without silence, our self-esteem weakens. We need it to create new eyes—to live.

Up there on the mountain, we learned that when silence speaks, we can begin to see with our other eyes, our spiritual eyes. As was his habit, Dad was on the mountain at first light each morning. It was on one of those mornings that he shared the magic of sunrise with me, opening my spiritual eyes, without saying a word.

We'd tied the horses off and made our way to the east brink of Wagon Road Ridge. Sitting there at an elevation of ten thousand feet, we could see the East Desert, the San Rafael Swell, all the way to the now-pale line separating earth and sky. Soon, almost unnoticed, the first harbinger of the coming day, soft silver shafts of light, thrust heavenward into the morning sky. In a ritual as old as time itself, the sun was coming up, bringing life to the mountain.

Again, almost unnoticed, the first rays of light give way to soft yellow and then brilliant orange, chasing the night from the morning sky as the sun peeked over the edge of our world, the eastern horizon. We sat there together, the man and the boy, as the fall sky gave the rising sun an orange/blood-red complexion through the early-morning haze.

Climbing into the saddle and turning to face the morning sun, Dad softly admonished, "If a man is so full of himself that he doesn't see something greater than himself in the journey of life, he has no life." A wise man, Marcel Proust, put it this way: "The true journey of discovery lies not in seeking new landscapes, but in having new eyes."

With silence, we hear the still, small voice that guides us on the journey of life. It is a spiritual presence that must be honored if we are to be right with ourselves and others. The voice speaks quietly. Its words are simple. If we haven't heard them, it's because we haven't learned to listen to silence as it speaks to our heart.

Classrooms of Life

You live, you learn, you move on.

AFTER THE KOREAN War, I came home and worked here and there, finally settling in somewhat with Hermansen's Roller Mill. Part of a four-man crew, I helped turn wheat into flour and helped process barley, corn, and oats into feed for livestock. We ran the grains through a steam chamber and then between two large steel cylinders, the grain going in as kernels and coming out looking somewhat like cornflakes.

Saturdays were busy days. That's when farmers and ranchers brought their truckloads of grain to the mill to be rolled. Rolled grain was easier to digest, better utilized by the animals, and provided better nutrition than whole grain in its natural state. While the farmers waited their turn to be served, they often gathered on the mill platform to share stories, talk business, reminisce, and philosophize.

The mill, like the Tyro Club, the Wise Bench, and Spencer Olsen's, Bill Nielsen's, and Dewey's service stations, was a classroom of life, a gathering place where everyone was both a teacher and a student. Every now and then, nuggets of wisdom found their way into the conversation.

The old mill once served as the home of what would become Snow College. Maybe that's why, if one listened closely, a life lesson could be gleaned. On one occasion, a customer ordered five sacks of flour. I carefully loaded the flour into the trunk of her car. Each fifty-pound cloth sack filled with flour sold for two dollars, and as I closed the trunk lid, the woman handed me a ten-dollar bill. "Thanks so much, young man!" she exclaimed. "Oh, and keep the change; you've been most helpful."

The lesson? Be grateful for kind words. Sincerely offered, they're priceless. Life was like that back then—not a lot of money, but lessons to be learned. Sometimes how we listen is more important than the fact that we listen at all.

At times, the conversation turned to loves lost or the breakup of a marriage. On those occasions, one Cobble Heaven resident and sage always offered the reason why. From Whiskey, we learned that one or the other parties to the breakup was "a brick shy of a full load." Or maybe "a quart low on the dipstick." It could have been because "the lights are on, but nobody's home."

"I don't know what she saw in him," Whiskey would often wonder. "He was on the back row asleep when looks and brains were handed out." On another occasion, Smiley Christensen, a bachelor, counseled, "Marriage is an old lesson from the School of Hard Knocks, which teaches men patience, long suffering, and a lot of stuff he wouldn't have to tolerate and learn if he only had the horse sense to stay single like me."

I'd worked at the mill a year and a half when the boss informed me, "Business is too slow to keep three men, so I'm going to have to let you, the last one hired, go." One door closes, another door opens. I took my last paycheck—I earned two dollars an hour—and walked up to the Bank of Ephraim, where I got a loan to pay for winter and spring quarters at Snow College. Married with a baby girl, I would use that last check to live on until the first GI Bill check arrived. That check, and the ones that would see me and my family through four years and a bachelor's degree, amounted to $140.

That experience in the "Classroom of Life" wasn't unique in that time and place. It was just one thread in the fabric that would shape a generation. When we hit a bump in the road, we reached out to each other and went on. We'd been through the Great Depression, World War II, and the Korean War, so we just worked, prayed, and moved on.

Returning Home

Where we love is home—home that our feet may leave,
but not our hearts.

—Oliver Wendell Holmes

When you grow up in a family with fourteen children, every special occasion takes on added significance. Not that these times are more important than they would be in a smaller family, but they come around more often, and you have more opportunity to experience life. Birthdays, high-school graduations, weddings, anniversaries, and new family members—they're celebrated once, twice, sometimes three times a month.

I've heard it said that you can tell what kind of home parents provided for their children by their kids' desire to return after they'd flown the coop. It's a truism, I think, that if someone loves you, that particular person can be set free only to return again and again. If that doesn't happen, the story goes, you never had that love in the first place.

Well, in my family, we all came home again and again. Like the river, our strength flowed from home, from our source.

It's both an art and a science to mold a young life into a loving, caring, responsible adult. I think big families help accomplish that. The glue of life's struggles keeps them together.

When a dozen or more family members gather for each meal, there's a lot of teamwork involved. My mother was like a traffic cop. Looking back, I have to marvel at the way she always seemed to adjust to the ebb and flow of her kids' lives.

We lived off the land, so soup, homemade bread, and potatoes and gravy with homegrown meat were the staples of our existence. Those things were kept at the ready in the big oven of the old woodburning stove for late arrivals. There was always enough for one more.

When Mom baked bread, which she did a couple of times a week, there just happened to be enough dough for two or three drippers of biscuits. When they came out of the oven, a big pitcher of cold milk along with butter and homemade jam and honey joined them on the big oak table. Everything there came by way of the sweat of the brow—through the labors, in one way or another, of every family member. We acknowledged the rewards involved in doing and contributing a fair share. Payday consisted of a crisp brown crust, hot out of the oven, saturated in freshly churned butter with a generous layer of apricot jam.

Hot bread fresh from the oven signified a time of conversation and laughter—a time that would build bonds so strong that years later, even though we'd been taught to stay close to one another, strong wings would take some of us to places with names we'd never imagined. I've heard it said that the stronger the wings, the farther from home a chick can safely fly. In that big family, we were given strong wings.

In those early years, I gave thanks to Mom and Dad and my brothers and sisters. But not often enough, not loudly enough. I'd like to be able to do that over. I'd like to relive those missed opportunities.

Mom recently celebrated her eighty-sixth birthday. I held her, kissed her, and told her I loved her. I don't know if she heard me. She sleeps a lot, and her eyes struggle to focus. Alzheimer's, they call it. I wish I could retrace my steps. I would have hugged her, kissed her, and said "I love you, Mom!" a lot more.

But I'm lucky; in a big family, you get lots of opportunities to say those things. I only wish I'd learned how to say them more. I've lost four sisters and my dad. Marlene was just sixteen—cancer. Lois was thirtysomething—complications from surgery. Georgia was sixty—heart attack. Suzy was forty-three—congestive heart failure. My dad was seventy-six—cancer.

In big families you get lots of opportunity to ask "Why?" when death comes calling. I wish I'd learned to say "I love you" more—to *show* love more.

Sometimes death is a compassionate caller who erases the pain of tired and broken bodies. Sometimes the time of its coming is clear, expected. On other occasions, it comes unannounced. I've experienced both. Neither is easy. It's about letting go. But we don't let go easily.

Letting go of Susan was a bittersweet experience. Suzy was given a huge load to carry in this life. She had a physical handicap that made her speech difficult to understand, and she was diagnosed as "uneducable" by the school system. She came home, and the years went by. In spite of being excluded from much of society, she learned and accomplished many things and always had a smile on her face. And a big family to love her.

Suzy was Mom's angel, and when Dad was gone, they carried on together until Mom was stricken with Alzheimer's. In her final days, Mom went to a care center, and Suzy went to a group home for the disabled where she earned thirty-four cents a day.

When Suzy left us, I took care of her personal affairs: signed the papers, paid the bills, put her life's possessions into a few boxes, and made sure each family member got something to remember her by. That was several years ago.

Three days ago, something cropped up and took me on the journey all over again. "Suzy," an employee at the Nephi Bank called to say, "had a savings account. Seventy-one dollars and ninety-six cents. Would you come and close it out?"

I was stunned by the news. But it figures. When you grow up in a big family and struggle for every possession, you value resources and hang on to any excess for a rainy day.

I put that money in Mom's account at the care center. I think Susan would have liked that—knowing she'd helped Mom, even in a very small way.

I had to dig out court documents to prove I was Susan's guardian before the bank would let me have the money. That offended me. I'd *always* been her guardian. We all were. It's that way in big families. It has to be to survive!

Along with the document, I found a copy of Susan's obituary. I sat speechless, lost in the silence of yesterday's memories. If I could retrace my steps back to earlier times, I'd force myself to find my tongue. Maybe I could have said something, done something, to brighten up her life, to see that others like her got the kind of help that's available today.

But I can't go back. None of us can. Instead, we can only try to move on as best we can, to let go only when we must. And then, like those in my big family who've won life's battles, let go gracefully, leaving behind a legacy born out of that family, out of that man and woman who gave us life's most precious gift—love. And like the waters of the river, the love from family flows on, feeding each growing generation from its source and making them one.

The Long Shadow of Love

The quest for love is a lifelong journey without a final destination.

I'VE BEEN AN orphan since January 19, 1996. That's the day she left us. Her family stood around her bed that morning as dawn broke in the eastern sky. She looked very small there—like a child. The breaths came hard now. Long pauses in between. Then silence. It was done. Her escape from her tortured body was complete. No more soul-wrenching gasps for life-sustaining oxygen.

One by one, we bent over the frail figure lying on the bed. When it was my turn, the lump in my throat choked off the words. "Mom...I don't...I don't...know how to say good-bye."

Now, several years later, I realize that I don't have to say good-bye at all. Yes, we're separated physically, but we're forever tied together spiritually.

In times of need, I still share my heart with her. It's funny now how she gave me answers and solutions to life's challenges before I'd need them. I find myself giving my kids and grandkids the same advice she gave me: "Find someone to share your heart with. Be at peace with yourself. Challenge yourself and keep growing. Say 'I love you' to your family every chance you get."

Over a life that spans some sixty-plus years, I've found that saying "I love you" opens hearts and influences who we are and what we do. It is the very essence of being. It dictates who we are in the eyes of family—and the world.

A few caring words—even though we may take it for granted that others know what we're thinking—can have enormous power if we take the opportunity to actually verbalize them. Three of the shortest words spoken by humans, "I love you," can cast an incredibly long shadow. Mom has been gone, in the physical sense, several years now. Yet her teaching, caring, and loving remain here with me.

Maybe that's how we achieve a part of what we call eternal life—by caring about someone enough to leave a part of us with them, in them. I'm convinced that this is so.

Love isn't something that just comes forth. And when it does come, it isn't intended to be turned on and off like the faucet in the kitchen sink.

It has to be built, like the house we live in, with a firm foundation and strong walls to shelter it from harm's way. It has to be watched over and cared for. Refurbished from time to time. Made new. Constant in both foul and fair weather.

I learned that, almost unknowingly at the time, from my mother's devotion to my father during his struggle with alcohol. Why she stayed and endured, only she knew—while the family wondered. The answer was simple but so profound that it eluded us until we had families of our own. She'd told him she loved him. Having put the conviction of her heart into words, there was no turning back.

And although Dad was tortured by the demons of alcohol for some twenty years, he found ways to reward her devotion. I have a crimson heart-shaped maple leaf sent by my father to my mother from Bonanza, Utah. It arrived in a small, white envelope, pressed between two pieces cut from the side of a cereal box. The words carefully printed there on the pressed leaf were: "To my wife—with all my love!"

We found the envelope and the leaf in the drawer of Mom's nightstand as we went through the old home after she was unable to remain there. The flap on the envelope was wrinkled and worn. She must have gone to that drawer often for support, for assurance, and for strength. Twenty-plus years alone, and the words still cast a long shadow—"with all my love!"

Even now, with Mom and Dad physically removed, I stand by who and what I am in the shadow of one woman's love. Eternal life? Eternal love? I'm convinced it is so! Love casts a long shadow!

Simply Speaking

Simply speaking, they aren't much.
Still, they speak of love.
And fluttering over time,
The heart they touch.

Crimson leaves inscribed
With words of love.
Crimson leaves—timeless reminders
Of one man and one woman's love.

Words of eternal love.
God's gift to us,
Sent from high above.

We found them there,
In the drawer next to her bed.
"To my wife—with all my love,"
They said.

Simply speaking, they aren't much.
Still, they speak of love.
And fluttering over time,
The heart they touch.

Travel Light

Attitude decides all *things!*

LIKE STONES CAST upon tranquil waters, the lessons of generations past ripple forth, giving substance and direction to those who follow.

Elmer was one of those men who, in his own quiet way, left his mark on the shoreline of life for those who knew him. He wore blue-denim bib overalls and walked with a distinctive limp, almost dragging one leg along. A sturdy hand-carved cane gave him support and balance. He came home from the Great War that way.

Elmer had seen more of life and death than most—more of the ugly side of life. On the surface, he had little to smile about. Still, that was one of his trademarks. He greeted everyone with a smile, and when parting, he'd say, "So long, travel light," with the same smile.

Like most who heard those words, I didn't give a lot of thought to their meaning until one day I happened to be in Scissors's barber shop as Elmer and another customer exchanged good-byes. As was his habit, Elmer smiled and said, "So long, travel light."

That was when Scissors, the barber, asked, "What does that mean? Travel light?"

A man of few words, Elmer hesitated before responding. "Don't worry yourself to an early grave."

To that Scissors countered, "Easier said than done."

"Ya," Elmer agreed, "but what's the sense of hanging on to life's problems?"

There's an old Ben Franklin adage about advice. To paraphrase, it says, "Wise men don't need it, and fools won't heed it." If you were to look at Elmer in his bib overalls, sweat-stained hat, and scuffed ankle-high shoes, it would be easy to dismiss out of hand anything he might say. However, truth is where you find it. And foolish or wise, it would be easy to miss out on the wisdom, the caring, and the concern conveyed in a few simple words: "Travel light."

When Scissors probed Elmer for an explanation, there was a second lesson, a life lesson, in the exchange. "What you see is not always what you get," Elmer said as the conversation ended. That second lesson would be slow to reveal itself, but it carried powerful wisdom about judging on the basis of appearance.

After all, here was a man who pretty much lived a quiet life. He had little money, held no outward claim to fame, and didn't fit in most social circles. So unless you looked past the initial image, it would be easy to discount anything he might offer.

That meant you wouldn't see his sacrifice for his country, for you and me, in the cane and the dragging leg he'd carried since the Battle of the Bulge. It meant you wouldn't see the bounty of his garden shared quietly with those in need. You would miss the pride of a well-kept yard and home. Also, you wouldn't know that his only means of travel was by foot.

He didn't go to church, so you wouldn't see the strength and trust he held for a loving Savior. And, maybe most important, you wouldn't have seen the devotion and love for a sick and aging mother who spent her final years in his care.

The things in life that hold real value don't cost money. They can't be bought or sold. They're as timeless as man himself. When it comes time to shed our mortal skin, we can take the fruits of love, sacrifice, and service with us—but not our earthly wealth.

Perhaps Alma 41:3 in the Book of Mormon said it best. "And it is requisite with the justice of God that men should be judged according to their works; and if their works were good in this life, and the desires of their hearts were good, that they should also, in the last day, be restored to that which is good."

That is the standard for judgment. It's simple and to the point. Still, doing good works and incorporating lofty desires into the heart are sometimes difficult to see when our focus is on worldly values—money, attire, social status. Elmer had little of those. What he *did* have was a promise that because of his goodness, he "should also, in the last day, be restored to that which is good."

Epilogue

We don't think or talk enough about where we came from and how our lives have been "gifted" by family, friends, and strangers—about how adversity often brings blessings into our lives. We need to do more of that, especially in these troubled times. I hope my stories have encouraged you to do that. I hope, too, that in reading *Gifting and the Stick,* you have found reason to smile now and then and perhaps experience a moment or two of personal reflection and gratitude as you recall experiences and people who have left you better than they found you.

Finally, thanks for reading *Gifting and the Stick.* My very best to you, and may your life be blessed in the "Gifting" way because you choose carefully "the Stick" promising those gifts. What we focus on, the stick we pick up, is what we will become.

Boyd Keisel

About the Author

Boyd Keisel is a writer, outdoorsman, and grandpa who grew up on a small farm near Ephraim, Utah, with thirteen brothers and sisters. Having served his country during the Korean War, Boyd was "gifted" with the GI Bill, which at $140 a month enabled him to earn a bachelor's degree in English and then a master's degree and an education specialist degree in school administration. Boyd served as a teacher, coach, principal, assistant superintendent, and superintendent over a long, rewarding career in public education. After retiring from public education, Boyd continued a lifelong relationship with the Native American people as the director of a program providing education opportunities to high school–aged Navajo students.

Readers desiring to contact Boyd may do so by email at mybkstories@gmail.com, where they are invited to make comments and share their own Gifting and the Stick experiences. Readers may also check out Boyd's website at mybkstories.com where they may get to know the author, see what his next project may be, and purchase copies of his book.

37527912R00075

Made in the USA
San Bernardino, CA
19 August 2016